Lloyd George Knew My Father

A Play

WILLIAM DOUGLAS HOME

SAMUEL  FRENCH

LONDON
NEW YORK   TORONTO   SYDNEY   HOLLYWOOD

LLOYD GEORGE KNEW MY FATHER

First performed under the title **Lady Boothroyd of the By-Pass** by the New Midland Theatre Company, Boston, on 1st February 1972, with the following cast of characters:

Lady Boothroyd (Sheila)	Patricia Leslie
Richardson	Iain Armstrong
General Sir William Boothroyd	Anthony Roye
William Boothroyd, M.P.	Arnold Peters
Maud Boothroyd	Joy Singlehurst
Sally Boothroyd	Penelope Anne Croft
Dickie Horton-Jones	Rayner Bourton
The Rev. Trevor Simmonds	Brian Weston

Designed and directed by Anthony Roye
Lighting by Lawrence Whitfield

Subsequently presented under the title **Lloyd George Knew My Father,** by Ray Cooney and John Gale, by arrangement with Hugh Wontner, on 4th July 1972, at the Savoy Theatre, London, with the following cast of characters:

General Sir William Boothroyd	Ralph Richardson
Lady Sheila Boothroyd	Peggy Ashcroft
Hubert Boothroyd, M.P.	James Grout
Maud Boothroyd	Janet Henfrey
Sally Boothroyd	Suzan Farmer
Simon Green	Simon Cadell
Rev. Trevor Simmonds	David Stoll
Robertson	Alan Barnes

The play directed by Robin Midgley
Setting by Anthony Holland
Lighting by Chris Ellis

The action of the play passes in the sitting-room of Boothroyd Hall, Sir William's home

ACT I
    Scene 1   Saturday morning
    Scene 2   Sunday morning

ACT II
    Scene 1   Sunday evening
    Scene 2   Monday morning

Time – the present

ACT I

SCENE 1

The living-room of Boothroyd Hall. Saturday morning

It is obviously the most comfortable room in the house. It is half male, half female furnished. In other words, it has bookcases, which give it the air of a library; deep armchairs, which give it the air of a female-frequented morning-room, or sitting-room. There are portraits of a few earlier Boothroyds, notable among them Sir Hubert, who clearly followed the same profession as the owner of the house. The panelling, the architecture, the obviously thick wall in which the window—or windows—is set, are typical of the kind of country house scattered through the southern half of England in the Civil War arena. Through the windows can be seen a garden, a lawn, and perhaps a grey wall with a herbaceous border in front of it, and at the end of the lawn there is (or would be if one could see it) a ha-ha leading into a field which rises on a pleasing contour to the woods beyond, a quarter of a mile away. It is, in fact, the kind of house in which Charles the First would, at some time, have stayed before a battle, and in the woods of which Charles the Second would have hidden in some well-leafed oak

As the CURTAIN *rises Sheila is discovered at the piano, playing scales. When she finishes the grandfather clock in the hall strikes eight. Robertson is setting Sheila's and William's eggs on their plates and their coffee-cups and saucers in their places. He props a letter, which is also on his serving trolley, against the toast-rack by William's place, then moves to Sheila*

Robertson Breakfast is served, my lady.
Sheila Thank you, Robertson. (*She stops playing*) You know about them going hunting, don't you?
Robertson Yes, my lady. Sandwiches for three.
Sheila That's right. And two here. That's unless there's any change of plan. (*She resumes playing*)

Sir William, who is very old and slow-moving, comes in through the hall, pauses by the clock to check his watch, then goes towards the breakfast table

(*As he passes her*) Good morning, William. (*She stops playing, takes off her spectacles, puts them in her pocket, and rises*)
William (*to Roberston*) What did she say?
Robertson Good morning, Sir William.
William Yes, yes. Never mind that. I asked what she said.

Sheila (*louder*) I said "Good morning, William". (*She tidies the music*)
William Oh, is that all! (*He glances at her, then out of the window*)

Robertson puts the newspaper by the table. Sheila looks out of the window

(*Sitting at the table*) Ten degrees, I shouldn't wonder, last night, Robertson?
Robertson No, only three, Sir William.
William That all? No damned good to anyone. Good morning, dear.

Robertson exits

Sheila (*kissing William*) Good morning, William.
William Must have been my eiderdown.
Sheila What must, dear?
William Made me think it froze much harder. It slipped off.
Sheila Why don't you tuck it in?
William I do. But it slips out again when I'm asleep. Worse than a snake. (*He picks up the letter*) Who's this from?
Sheila (*sitting*) How should I know, dear?
William I know the writing, but I'm damned if I can place it.
Sheila Why not open it and see? (*She opens the "Advertiser"*)
William Yes, good idea. (*He starts to open it*)
Sheila (*coming on something in the "Advertiser"*) I knew it!
William Knew what?
Sheila Do stop chattering—I'm reading.
William (*with the letter now open*) It's from Gerald, and he's asked us out to lunch on Monday.

There is no reply as Sheila is engrossed in what she has seen in the paper

Sheila . . .
Sheila Yes, dear?
William Gerald's asked us out to lunch on Monday.
Sheila So you said.
William Well, are we going?
Sheila No.
William Why not?
Sheila Because I won't be here on Monday.
William What?
Sheila I won't be here on Monday.
William Oh? Oh well, filthy food and a damned draughty house. But still, I like old Gerald. Known him since the First War—went through Sandhurst and the Dardanelles together. Sandhurst was the most uncomfortable. Well, what am I to say to him?
Sheila You don't believe me, do you?
William (*buttering toast*) Yes, my dear, of course.
Sheila You don't! You think I'm bluffing. But I'm not. I said I would the first day that the scheme was mooted, didn't I—last February?
William Yes, dear.

Sheila At this very table. We were having breakfast—when I saw it in the *Advertiser*, and I said: "William, if that scheme goes through, I won't be here to see it."

William Yes, dear.

Sheila Well, it's gone through. Listen. (*She reads from the paper*) "Bypass link to run through Boothroyd Park. On Monday morning, first thing, eight o'clock to be precise, the first sod will be cut by Mr Bertie Gray's bulldozer. Mr Gray has driven for the County Council since he left the Armoured Corps in nineteen blah—(*She skips a bit*)—At Mr Hubert Boothroyd, M.P's meeting in the Town Hall last week-end in answer to a questioner who asked him how much compensation his father General Sir William Boothroyd had received"—what cheek!—"the Member answered: 'Quite fair, but I haven't got the figure, to be frank with you.'" Well, that's a lie, to start with.

William Yes, Hubert fixed the whole caboodle.

Sheila I'll tell you something, William—Hubert's never tried to stop it!

William Nonsense, my dear.

Sheila Well, he may have done before the General Election, but not after it. He saw which way the wind was blowing, after all those recounts, and he caved in. Oh, how I hate politicians. (*She bangs the top of her egg with her spoon*)

William Lloyd George was worse than Hubert.

Sheila Well, he was a Liberal.

William Came out to G.H.Q. in 'seventeen when I was on the Staff. You should have seen the fellow! Hair below his collar. And a flapping cloak. Looked like a well-stuffed vulture. It's all in my diaries in the study.

Sheila Yes, dear, I know.

William Ought to get them published some time.

Sheila Well, we have tried, haven't we, dear?

William Not for ages.

Sheila Well, three years ago. We gave them to that charming son-in-law of Fatty Cavan's, that week-end in Gloucestershire, remember?

William Turned 'em down flat, didn't he?

Sheila Yes, I'm afraid so, William.

William Damned cheek! I was thinking in my bath last night, that I must be the only general this century who hasn't had his diaries published. When is Hubert coming?

Sheila Hubert's here, dear. And Maud. And Sally, and Sally's young man.

William When did they arrive?

Sheila Late last night.

William Thought they hadn't dined here. Don't remember being that bored!

Sheila They're going hunting today.

William Oh, yes. What am I to say to Gerald?

Sheila Anything you like, dear!

William I can't ring the fellow up and say you're doing yourself in on Monday morning, so we can't come.

Sheila Why not?

William Well, it sounds damned silly.

Sheila Well then, ring him up and say you'll go.

William Alone?

Sheila You'll be alone in any case.

William Oh.

Sheila Filthy food there—or a cold lunch here—what's left from Sunday supper—that's the choice. So, make up your mind.

William What're you looking at?

Sheila You, William.

William (*feeling his tie*) Why? What's wrong?

Sheila There's nothing wrong. But it's amazing how one just takes things for granted, isn't it? I don't suppose I've looked at you at breakfast once since nineteen-twenty-two.

William (*lowering his head to avoid her scrutiny*) Let's have the sugar.

Sheila (*passing the sugar bowl*) Nineteen-twenty-two. How many breakfasts is that?

William Damned if I know.

Sheila Well, let's work it out. (*She puts on her spectacles, takes a pencil from her pocket and writes on the "Advertiser"*) Three-sixty-five times fifty. O. Five, carry two, Five sixes—thirty. Plus the two—that's thirty-two. And carry three. Five three's is fifteen—add the three—that's eighteen—one, eight, two, five, O. Nearly twenty thousand breakfasts since we married, William, you and I.

William grunts and goes on eating

Don't just grunt. That's a lot of breakfasts. Forty thousand boiled eggs. That's a lot of boiled eggs, William.

William ignores, or does not hear, this, so she repeats it, louder

Forty thousand boiled eggs.

William What about them?

Sheila That's a lot of boiled eggs. And do you know, only one of them was bad. That was in Oban, when we took that fishing, the year that Prince Charles was born.

William I had a bad one the week-end we stayed with Gerald for the Hunter Trials.

Sheila Oh yes—so you did. Still, even so, I think that we've been very lucky.

Hubert comes in dressed for hunting, in red coat, etc., carrying his riding cap which he puts on a bust on the drinks table before moving to look out of the window

Hubert 'Morning, Mother.

Sheila Oh, good morning, Hubert.

Hubert Good morning, Father.

William 'Morning, Hubert. Where's the Meet?

Hubert At Shenstone Gorse.

William Right on the boundary, by Jove . . .

Hubert You're telling me. We ought to get a move on. Sally had her breakfast yet?

Sheila No, dear.

Hubert Oh lord! Maud's just coming. Any news?

Sheila The proper papers haven't come yet.

Hubert Anything in there about my speech?

Sheila Yes. I've been reading it. Work on the bypass starts on Monday morning.

Hubert So they tell me.

William Has Birdie been fed yet?

Sheila No, I shouldn't think so. Hubert, did you see the Minister of Transport last week?

Hubert Rather! Bought him a drink. Two, in fact. He wouldn't budge, though.

Sheila Did you really try to make him?

Hubert Like hell.

Sheila What did he say?

Hubert Nothing doing.

Sheila Did you tell him Charles the First stayed here the night before the Battle of Edgehill?

Hubert No.

Sheila Why not, dear?

Hubert I didn't think it relevant.

Sheila But it's the whole point. Don't you realize he sat here, having breakfast, looking out across that very field, and now it's going to be bisected by a dual carriageway?

Hubert You'll never see it from here, Mother—with the cutting.

Sheila That is not the point. And anyway, we'll hear it—at least, I won't, but your father will, and Maud and Sally.

Hubert In a north-east gale, perhaps—not otherwise. And south-west's the prevailing wind here. Anyway, why won't you hear it? You aren't half as deaf as Father.

William She'll be dead, my boy, that's why.

Hubert It won't take that long, Mother! Are you coming to the Meet, Papa?

William When are you starting?

Hubert Half an hour.

Sheila I won't be here on Monday morning, Hubert.

William When the first sod drives his bulldozer into the . . .

Sheila Be quiet, William. I'm afraid your father doesn't take me seriously, Hubert. I can only hope that you will.

Hubert Of course, Mother. Monday morning, where're you going?

Sheila That is not for me to say.

Hubert Well, I'll be catching the eight-twenty, if that's any good to you.

Sheila No, I'll be gone by eight.

Hubert (*exchanging a look with William*) By car, you mean?

Sheila No, I don't.

Hubert Sorry, Mother, I don't get you.

Sheila Never mind, you soon will. Have you got no sense of history? Look! (*She points at a portrait*) Your ancestor, Sir Hubert Boothroyd, sat here with his King three hundred years ago, and looked out on that field that James the First had given to his father.

Hubert (*looking at William*) Where are we now, Mother? Back at Edge-hill?

Sheila Where Sir Hubert died, yes. Two hours later! After his last breakfast.

William Fell into a pond, poor fellow. Did you know that, Sheila?

Sheila Yes, dear.

William Horse reared up and dumped him in a duckpond, and his armour filled with water, and he went down like an old tobacco tin—gug-gug-gug-guggle-guggle—(*after a pause*)—gug.

Sheila Well, anyway, he died for something he believed in.

William Yes, poor devil—had no option.

Sheila And you don't care, Hubert—do you?

Hubert I do, Mother. I feel very sorry for him. But it's damn-all to do with the bypass.

Sheila Please don't swear at breakfast.

Hubert Sorry, Mother.

Sheila And it's everything to do with it. This is the first time that a yard of Boothroyd land's been stolen, and the Government have damn-all right to steal it. James the First left Boothroyd to Sir Hubert's father in —in . . . '

William Pretty shady circumstances, if you ask me.

Sheila (*getting the word*) Perpetuity—yes. And it's been in perpetuity now for three hundred years.

Hubert The Government are paying compensation, Mother.

Sheila Never mind that. It's the thin edge of the wedge. It'll be the field this year, and then the garden—then the house! One can't call anything one's own these days. You never know when someone in a bowler hat and pin-striped trousers isn't going to come and steal your birthright.

Hubert It's not stealing, Mother. It's legitimate.

Sheila I don't care.

Hubert Possibly not. But that doesn't change the fact.

Sheila The fact is that you ought to have resigned.

Hubert Resigned! What for?

Sheila It would have been a gesture.

Hubert And a pretty silly one! I'm sorry, Mother, but it would. Just putting up another marginal to auction.

Sheila All you think about's your beastly seat. How I hate politicians!

William Lloyd George was the worst I ever saw. Came out to G.H.Q. in 'seventeen, when I was on the staff.

Sheila Yes, dear, you told me.

William Dare say. But I didn't tell you, Hubert, Hair over his collar. I can see him now, the little monkey. Telling Haig his job. If I had been Haig I'd have kicked him up the backside. It's all in my diaries in the study.

Ought to get them published some time. Did you say you'd given them to Fatty Cavan's son-in-law? (*He starts to busy himself with the fly-box, working on the "Hairy Mary"*)

Sheila Three years ago, yes, dear.

William He must have turned them down, then. Damned cheek! (*To Hubert*) Well, what time are you starting?

Hubert In ten minutes.

William Anything on today, dear?

Sheila Only *Grandstand*.

William All right, I'll come. I can finish off this "Hairy Mary" tonight. Are you coming, Sheila?

Sheila No, I've got a lot of things to see to here. But you go.

Hubert If you're coming to the Meet we'll take you in our car, then when the hunt's on you can follow the hounds in it. It's like yours to drive.

Sheila Be careful of the horses, dear.

William They won't be with me. They'll be in the horse-box.

Sheila I'll ring for Robertson and order you some sandwiches. (*She exchanges a look with Hubert then goes to the bell*)

Hubert When are you going fishing, Father?

William I hope Gerald asks us, same as last year.

Hubert I'm still not clear where you're going to on Monday morning, Mother.

Sheila That makes two of us!

William She's doing herself in, Hubert.

Hubert Ha, ha! Very funny.

William When the first sod . . .

Sheila Be quiet, William.

Hubert Well, I wouldn't try your little joke on Maud. You know what she's like.

Sheila It is not a joke.

Hubert Well, joke or not, she might believe you.

Sheila That's what you'll all have to do.

Robertson comes in

Oh, Robertson, the General is going with the others, to the Meet. And he'll be staying out, so could you ask your wife to make a few more sandwiches and p'raps a piece of cake, and a cheese biscuit.

Robertson Yes, my lady.

William Don't forget my flask.

Robertson Sir! Mr Saunderson just rang to say that he'll be dropping in the parcel on his way by.

Sheila Thank you, Robertson. He is the one who made the greenhouse, isn't he?

Robertson That's right, my lady.

Sheila Well, he did that very nicely.

Robertson goes

Hubert Saunderson's the village undertaker, Mother.

Sheila Yes, I know. That's why I've been in touch with him. I've got a little job for him.

Hubert You're going too far, Mother.

Sheila In what way, dear?

Hubert People talk, Mama.

Sheila I'm sorry, Hubert, but I like to plan ahead.

William Quite right. Damned politicians never plan ahead. Just live from hand to mouth. Our hands! Their mouths!

Maud enters dressed for hunting, carrying a whip and gloves. She goes to Sheila and gives her a kiss

Maud Good morning, all.

Sheila Good morning, Maud.

William Good morning, Maud.

Hubert Sally dressed yet?

Maud Nearly.

Hubert We'll be late if we don't get a move on. Come on.

Maud Are you coming, Sheila?

Sheila No, but William is.

Maud I don't think Sally's young man wants to come—would you mind looking after him?

Sheila No. I'd be delighted. I'm sure he's nice.

Hubert Humph!

William What does the fellow do?

Hubert He's a reporter.

William Good God! What rag does he write for?

Maud He's a freelance.

Sheila Really, at his age. That's very go-ahead.

Hubert I doubt if any decent newspaper'd have him.

William Wonder if he'd like to see my diaries?

Sheila Yes, I'm sure he would, dear.

William Great War and the last do.

Maud Perhaps he'll get them published for you.

William Not a hope. I tried that son-in-law of Kitchener's.

Sheila No, Cavan's, dear.

William What? Oh, yes, Cavan's. Wouldn't touch them. Said they were too personal. I told him: "That's the point of diaries, isn't it?" And he said: "No. The point of diaries is to keep 'em to yourself."

Maud Well, Hubert's got a good spread in the *Advertiser*, Sheila.

Sheila Yes, dear, so I've just been reading.

Maud You don't sound too pleased.

Hubert She isn't. She thinks I've let down the family.

Maud You? How?

Hubert By not stopping the bypass going through the Park.

Maud You did your best, though.

Sheila Ha, ha!

Hubert I know, but she thinks I ought to gallop out on Monday morning, and do battle like Sir Hubert did at Edgehill.
William Maudie know about him?
Sheila Yes, I'm sure she does.
Maud Who?
William Old Sir Hubert. That's him up there. (*He indicates the picture*)
Maud Killed at Edgehill, wasn't he?
William That's right, yes—but do you know how?
Maud Do I, Hubert?
Hubert Yes, of course you do. He fell into a duck pond.
Maud Yes, of course.
William His horse reared up and dumped him.
Maud Oh, yes, I remember.
William And his armour filled with water, and he went down like an old tobacco tin—gug—guggle—guggle—(*he pauses*)—gug.
Maud How dreadful.

Robertson enters with the flask and a string-tied box on a silver salver

Robertson Your flask, sir.
William What? Oh, yes—thank you.
Hubert Go and chase Miss Sally down, please, Robertson.
Robertson Sir! Your parcel, my lady. Mr Saunderson just dropped it.
Sheila Thank you. (*She unpacks the parcel of coffin wood samples*)

Robertson starts to move away

   Robertson——
Robertson My lady?
Sheila —it's your afternoon off, isn't it, today?
Robertson That's right, my lady.
Sheila Well, you'll have to do the job this morning. I'd like a hole dug in the rough grass just beyond the croquet lawn.
Robertson What sort of hole, my lady?
Sheila A grave, Robertson.
Robertson A grave, my lady? Has the budgerigar conked out, then?
Sheila You're on the wrong tack, Robertson. I want a proper grown-up grave.
Robertson You mean a human grave, my lady?
Sheila That's right, Robertson. And please don't start until I've shown you the exact spot. There're a lot of bulbs there.
Robertson Very good, my lady.

Robertson exits, throwing a look at Hubert and William en route

William Well, you couldn't have picked on a better fellow if you'd called for volunteers. He did the job in all my campaigns. No damned good at fighting. Graves, latrines, latrines and graves. Graves and latrines . . .
Sheila Yes, dear. You've made the point.

William He got the M.M. for it, too—worked like a Trojan. Robertson'll do you proud, dear.

Maud Have I woken up yet?

Hubert Mother's being difficult this morning.

William Sheila's doing herself in first thing on Monday morning, when the first sod . . .

Sheila William! (*Holding out the samples to Hubert*) What do you think of these, dear?

Hubert What are they?

Sheila Sample wood for coffins.

Maud reacts

Which do you like best, dear?

Maud Take them away, Sheila. I can't bear that sort of thing.

Sheila Don't be so silly, dear. You're far too old to behave like an ostrich. I like this one best. (*To Hubert*) Don't you? It's oak.

Hubert I'm sorry. I'm not interested.

Sheila You will be one day, even if you're going to be cremated. William, what do you think?

William What's that, my dear?

Sheila Which of these do you like best?

William I don't like any of them. What the devil are they?

Sheila Sample wood for coffins. (*Pointing*) I like this one best.

William I'll bet it's damned expensive.

Sheila So it ought to be—it's oak.

Hubert Don't leave them there when that young man comes down.

Sheila Why not? They might be panelling. Now, William, go and get your things on, or you'll be late. Put on your warmest muffler.

William Why? There's a heater in the car.

Sheila I dare say, but you're bound to get out at the Meet to chase the cherry brandy. Do as you're told.

William Right, my dear. What am I to say to Gerald about lunch on Monday?

Sheila I've already told you, William. I can't make up your mind for you.

William You've been doing it for the last fifty years, my dear.

Sheila Well, that's all over now.

William A pity. (*To Hubert*) What time are we on parade?

Hubert Now, Father.

William I'll be there.

William goes

Maud You can't be serious.

Sheila I am, dear. Never more so in my life.

Maud I think it's very selfish of you.

Sheila Selfish!

Maud Yes. You're only thinking of yourself.

Sheila Myself! I'm fighting for the Boothroyds—now that they've **gone**

soft! Somebody's got to, and your husband won't. And William's much too old, and much too ga-ga.

Maud It'll cost Hubert the seat.

Sheila You're just as bad as he is. All you think about is his beastly seat.

Maud Well, Hubert's done a great deal for the county.

Sheila I dare say. He's done for Boothroyd Park, though.

Maud That was not his fault.

Hubert Go and chase Sally down, please, darling.

Maud All right, Hubert.

Maud goes out angrily

Hubert You've upset her, Mother. She admires me.

Sheila Well, it's nice to think that someone does, dear. Anyway, she's upset me, calling me selfish. I suppose Joan of Arc was selfish, too?

Hubert You're older than she was, and should know better. Well, I'm off now, Mother.

Sheila I can't say I'm sorry.

Hubert And please—don't try out your little joke on Sally. She's at an impressionable age.

Sheila Well, that'll be a change!

Hubert And not a word to that young man. Remember he's a journalist.

Sheila (*after a long pause*) I won't forget, I promise.

Hubert Good. Because they can't be trusted. Tell him Robertson's an archaeologist, or something.

Sally enters, unconventionally dressed for hunting

Sally Good morning, Grannie darling. (*She kisses Sheila*)

Sheila Good morning, dear.

Hubert Humph! About time.

Sally Good morning, Daddy. (*She kisses Hubert*) Sorry I'm late, I was trying to wake Simon.

Hubert (*noticing her riding outfit*) What on earth do you think you're wearing?

Sally Don't you like it?

Hubert It looks utterly ridiculous.

Hubert puts on on his riding cap and exits, closing the doors

Sally gets a clean cup from the trolley and pours herself some coffee

Sally What was Daddy saying when I came in, Grannie?

Sheila Quite a lot of things.

Sally No—about Simon.

Sheila Never mind, dear.

Sally Be nice to him, Sheila. He's sweet.

Sheila Are you going to marry him?

Sally Well, unofficially, yes. But I haven't told the parents yet.

Sheila When are you going to?

Sally Oh, I don't know—when the moment's ripe. I don't think Daddy likes him.

Sheila Why not?

Sally Well, for one thing because he's a journalist—and for another, he's not a Conservative.

Sheila What is he, then?

Sally I don't think anything.

Sheila Your father said I mustn't tell you something—so I'm going to.

Sally Good for you!

Sheila The reason being that I don't think children should be coddled, and because I think you've every right to know about the family.

Sally Has Grandfather gone round the bend?

Sheila No, dear—no farther round than usual. No, it's me. I've told your father and your mother and your grandfather, and now I'm telling you. I'm doing myself in on Monday morning.

Sally Go on!

Sheila *You* believe me, then?

Sally Of course. You wouldn't say so if you weren't going to, would you? But you've stood it for so long, why give in now?

Sheila Stood what?

Sally Well, Grandfather.

Sheila Sally!

Sally I'm sorry, Sheila. Well, what is it, then?

Sheila The bypass.

Sally Oh, I see. But what good will it do if . . .

Sheila It might stop them making it.

Sally But no-one knows what you're up to, do they?

Sheila Yes, your grandfather, your father and your mother—and you.

Sally But that's not enough. (*After a pause*) Grannie, I've got an idea.

Sheila Yes, dear, so have I.

Hubert (*off*) Come on, Sally!

Sally Coming.

Hubert (*off*) I want your help with the horses.

Sally (*collecting her hat*) Look after Simon for me, will you?

Sally runs out, leaving the door half open

Sheila puts the coffin samples on the sofa table, clears Maud's breakfast things to the trolley, then comes to the piano, selects a piece of music, and plays a "Funeral March"

Simon enters unseen, watches for a moment, then starts to turn away. Sheila. having got bored with the Funeral March, breaks into "Chopsticks". Simon, surprised, turns back, comes into the room, puts his camera down on the table and clears his throat. Sheila turns to him

Sheila Oh, I'm so sorry. How long have you been here?
Simon Since last night.
Sheila You must be Sally's young man.
Simon Simon Green, yes. And you must be Sally's grandmother.
Sheila Yes. Sheila Boothroyd.
Simon (*shaking hands*) Hello.
Sheila (*going towards the trolley*) Coffee?
Simon Yes, please. Black, please.
Sheila Sugar?
Simon Thank you.
Sheila One or two?
Simon Three, please.
Sheila You know your own mind, anyway. An egg? Toast?
Simon No, thanks, just the coffee.
Sheila So you're a journalist.
Simon Yes, freelance.
Sheila It sounds so romantic, doesn't it? Like some strange knight arriving at a tournament to find that the other jousts have been rigged. Do you get well paid?
Simon Yes, sometimes. When I get a scoop.
Sheila And is that often?
Simon Just depends if one's in luck. I got my first one last week.
Sheila How exciting.
Simon P'raps you saw the pictures? All the Sundays carried them.
Sheila I'm sure I did.
Simon A pile-up on the A1. Sixteen cars all concertina'd. I was driving down from Stamford, and I came right into it. So all I had to do was get my pictures. Two on fire, and seven ambulances.
Sheila Fancy!
Simon No one dead, though.
Sheila Oh dear. Well, one can't have everything. Are you a good photographer?
Simon Not too bad. It's my camera though, really—not me—foolproof.
Sheila And you're engaged to Sally, as I understand?
Simon Oh—who from?
Sheila Sally.
Simon (*relieved*) Oh, I see. Well, unofficially, yes.
Sheila When's it going to be official?
Simon When I've made a lot more cash. And when I think her father's coming round to me. What do you think of him?
Sheila My son?
Simon (*having forgotten*) Oh, sorry! Yes, of course.
Sheila Not much. He tends towards pomposity, don't you agree?
Simon They all do.
Sheila They?
Simon M.P.s.
Sheila Yes, I suppose so—broadly speaking. Some more coffee?
Simon Thanks.

Sheila pours coffee for him

You've got a lovely place here.
Sheila Isn't it.
Simon Built about sixteen hundred?
Sheila Yes, almost exactly. How observant of you. James the First gave
it to him. (*She points at the picture*) In perpetuity. Or to his father,
actually.
Simon (*getting up*) He looks a bit like Sally's father.
Sheila Do you think so? They're very different characters. Do sit down.

Simon sits

Sir Hubert died at Edgehill—had a little trouble with his horse, accord-
ing to my husband, but I'm sure he'll tell you all about it himself. So
you're interested in history?
Simon Yes, I am.
Sheila Then I'm quite sure you'd like to know that Charles the First had
breakfast here the morning of the battle.
Simon Really? (*He goes to put his cup down, pushing the coffin samples to
one side on the table*)
Sheila (*pointing*) Coffin samples.
Simon What?
Sheila Samples of different woods for coffins. Which do you like best?
Simon I don't like any of them much.
Sheila You mustn't be so squeamish. (*Bending and pointing*) I like this one
best, don't you?
Simon Yes—not bad.
Sheila Not bad! It's quite beautiful. It's oak. Came from the Park, I
shouldn't wonder.
Simon Very nice, yes.
Sheila I'm so glad you like it.
Simon Does your husband make them for a hobby?
Sheila William? Oh dear, no.
Simon Then why?
Sheila The undertaker in the village brought them up this morning, so
that I could choose one.
Simon May I ask who for?
Sheila Myself. Oh dear, I've let the cat out of the bag now, but I'm sure
you'd like another scoop. Not so potentially exciting as the A1, I'm
afraid. Much more parochial. I'm doing myself in on Monday morning.
Simon Really!
Sheila So you're interested?
Simon Yes.
Sheila Would you like to know why?
Simon Yes, please.
Sheila It's the bypass.
Simon "It's the bypass."
Sheila Yes, I said I'd do it if they did it, and they're doing it, so so am I.

Simon Of course.

Sheila I'm not mad. I'm as sane as you are. If I'd been mad, Sally would've warned you. She'd have said: "Beware of Grandma, as she's barking."

Simon (*with a chuckle*) She did say that, actually. But not about you. About your husband.

Sheila Oh, William. Yes, he isn't everyone's idea of sanity—especially the young's. But he's extremely old, and very deaf, and I'm afraid that Mr Lloyd George was very much to blame. Do you know anything about him?

Simon Only what you've told me, and what Sally said.

Sheila Not William—Lloyd George.

Simon I know the song.

Sheila The song?

Simon Well, "Lloyd George knew my father . . ."

Sheila Did he? Oh, you must tell William.

Simon No—that's what the song's called.

Sheila Oh, I see. How does it go?

Simon Just like that.

Sheila "Lloyd George knew my father"?

Simon And "My father knew Lloyd George", sung to the tune of "Onward, Christian Soldiers".

Sheila William'll adore that. Do you think he could learn it?

Simon Well, there isn't much to learn.

Sheila You mean that's really all?

Simon Yes.

Sheila Sing it to me. (*She goes to the piano*) And I'll play the tune. And ring the bell first. Over there, dear.

Simon rings the bell

Thank you. Now then. (*She sits at the piano*) Are you ready?

Simon Yes.

Sheila plays an opening bar or two, and then Simon starts singing

Simon (*singing*) "Lloyd George knew my father,
My father knew Lloyd George.
Lloyd George knew my father," etc.

As Simon is singing Robertson enters and stands looking astonished

Sheila Oh, Robertson, you can clear.

Robertson Very good, my lady. (*He starts clearing the breakfast things on to his tray, but leaves one or two items, including William's whisky flask*)

Sheila I'm so sorry. Shall we go on?

Simon Right.

They sing again. Robertson looks bewildered, but goes on clearing. Sheila and Simon sing a whole verse together. Simon stops, but Sheila goes on, so Simon joins in again

Sheila (*stopping*) Excuse me.

Simon Yes?

Sheila When does it end?

Simon It doesn't. We do. Any time we like.

Sheila I see. William's going to love that. Do you think you could teach it to him?

Simon I should think so.

Sheila Would you like to take a photograph of me beside the grave?

Simon The grave?

Sheila Yes. In among the daffodils. Robertson's just going to dig it for me, aren't you, Robertson?

Robertson Yes, very good, my lady.

Sheila Mr Green could give you a hand with it, if you like.

Robertson Thanks very much, sir.

Still more bewildered, Robertson picks up his tray and goes

Sheila If it gets into the papers you'll be suspected and my son is going to like you even less than he does now.

Simon If possible.

Sheila Which do you want most, a scoop—or Sally?

Simon Both.

Sheila Well said.

Simon I'll check the camera.

Sheila And I'll ring Mr Saunderson. (*She lifts the receiver, but hears William approaching and replaces it*)

William enters in an overcoat, bowler and woolly muffler

William Ah, there you are, dear.

Sheila William, this is Simon Green.

William Good God! I thought you were a girl.

Simon Sorry to disappoint you, sir.

William That's damned good. Did you hear that, Sheila?

Sheila Yes, dear.

William How did it go?

Simon What, sir?

William What you said.

Simon Sorry to disappoint you.

William That's it. Damned good. Ha, ha. Missed conscription, didn't you?

Simon Conscription? Oh, conscription. Yes, sir, by a long way.

William Pity. They'd have had that hair cut for you.

Simon So my grandfather keeps telling me.

William Your grandfather? Who's he?

Simon General Duggan.

William Duggan?

Simon That's right, sir.

William Did you say Duggan?
Simon Yes, sir.
William Dirty Duggan?
Simon General Sir Richard Duggan, sir.
William That's him. That's Dirty. He's your grandfather?
Simon That's right, sir. On my mother's side.
William Good God! You hear that, Sheila?
Sheila Yes, dear.
William Dirty Duggan. We fought right through the First War together,
    till they took us prisoner, and then we shared a tent together, no damned
    soap, and precious little water. Looked just like you, now I come to
    think of it! By Jove, yes—spitting image! Hence the nickname. Are you
    in the Army, too?
Simon No, I'm a journalist.
William Oh, yes, that's right. I've got diaries in the study. Great War—
    and this last do. I'd like to show them to you.
Simon I'd like to see them, sir.
William I'll go and get 'em out. I'd love to get 'em published. Gave them
    to some fellow once—who was it, Sheila?
Sheila Lady Cavan's son-in-law.
William Yes, that's right. Fatty Cavan's widow's son-in-law. Was he a
    publisher?
Sheila Yes, William.
William That's right. That's what gave us the idea, of course. (*To Simon*)
    He turned 'em down flat.
Simon Oh, I'm sorry.
William Never mind. I'll get 'em out. You never know your luck.
Simon Can I give you a hand, sir?
William No, they're exercise books. That's all, exercise books.

Hubert enters, dressed for the hunt and carrying his whip

Hubert Do come along, Father, for Heaven's sake.
William Yes, yes, I'm coming. This young fellow wants to see my diaries.

William exits

Hubert looks at his watch

Simon (*to Hubert*) Going hunting?
Hubert (*noticing the coffin samples and picking them up*) Mother, I'll take
    care of these. I'll put them in a safe place. (*To Simon*) They're samples
    for a wardrobe.

Hubert goes

Simon and Sheila smile at this

Simon I'll need some more film.

Sheila Will you get them to the papers in time?

Simon Yes, if I can get them to the station before lunch.

Sheila (*going to the phone*) Well, hurry.

Simon goes

Sheila dials a number

Sheila (*into the phone*) Is that you, Mr Saunderson? . . . Oh, good. It's Lady Boothroyd speaking. I've decided on the oak. . . . Yes, that's right. Now about the headstone. Could I come down to your brother-in-law's yard some time tomorrow morning just to have a look round?

Robertson enters to clear the remaining things to the trolley and take the tablecloth off the breakfast table

Oh, how nice. What time would suit him, do you think? . . . Perfect. Thank you so much. I'll look forward to that quite enormously. Good morning. (*She hangs up*) Robertson, I think we'll go and site the grave now, and Mr Green will help you with the digging.

Robertson Very good, my lady.

Williams enters with a hatbox full of exercise books in a poor state

William Sheila . . .

Sheila Yes?

William I might bump into Gerald at the Meet.

Sheila Well, that'll be nice for you.

William But what shall I tell him about lunch on Monday?

Sheila Tell him we'll telephone tomorrow.

William Good idea. Damned good idea. And don't get up to anything while I'm away.

Sheila Of course not, William.

William And give up that crazy idea. Or I'll have you certified.

Sheila You'd have a job. You're battier than I am, William.

William Not much in it, I'd say, dear. Six of one and half-dozen of the other.

Simon enters with more film for his camera

Simon Right! I've got enough film now.

William Ah! There you are, young fellow. Now, the diaries. Mice have been at them a bit, but not too badly. (*Indicating that Simon should join him, he moves to the sofa*)

Sheila Not now, William. Simon wants to see the garden.

William Garden? What the devil for?

Simon Don't worry, sir. I'll read them later.

Sheila Come along, dear. Robertson!

Robertson My lady.

Sheila, Robertson and Simon go

William sits on the sofa and opens his box. He looks in, then shuts the box rapidly. He opens it again just enough to get his hand inside and feels round. Eventually he locates a mouse

William Got you! (*He brings up his hand with a mouse in it. With his left hand he pours a little coffee in a saucer then brings it towards his right hand*) Come on, old chap —(*coaxingly*)—you'll find this more digestible than diaries.
Hubert (*off; shouting*) Come on, Dad.
William Right, my boy. We're coming.

William puts the mouse in his pocket and goes out, as—

the CURTAIN *falls*

SCENE 2

The same. Sunday, 10.40 a.m.

The breakfast table has gone

When the CURTAIN rises Sheila is discovered sitting on the sofa, trimming with a pair of scissors a piece of white card she has fashioned into the shape of a tombstone with a cross on top. She holds it away from her to check the shape. William enters

William Sheila! Sheila! You got any cash for the collection?
Sheila Yes, I think so—in my bag. (*She looks round for her bag*)
William (*interrupting her*) And don't forget that we're going to ring up Gerald about lunch tomorrow.
Sheila Yes, dear. Later.
William What am I to say to him?
Sheila It all depends, dear.
William What on?
Sheila Lots of things. Now, where's . . .
William Well, let's hope we'll know soon. It's not fair to keep the poor fellow on tenterhooks. You'll be late for church if you don't go and get your hat on.
Sheila I don't think I'll go this morning. I've a lot of letters to write.
William Who to? (*He goes to the bookcase and looks in it*)
Sheila Mostly tradesmen. We've got so few friends left, when you come to think of it—apart from Gerald and the Vicar. What are you looking for?
William Something to read during the sermon.

Sheila And besides, I've an appointment in the village.

William Who with?

Sheila Oh dear, I forget his name. But he's the husband of the sister of the man who made the greenhouse.

William Saunderson.

Sheila No—that's the man who made the greenhouse.

William That's what I said.

Sheila Oh, I see. Yes. But his brother-in-law's name's different. He makes gravestones. He's a stonemason. (*She goes to William with the card and a large envelope which she gets from the sofa table*) I've been working on the inscription. Shall I read it to you.

William Right. Let's have it.

Sheila (*reading*) "Sheila Jane—Beloved Wife of William Boothroyd." Then the dates. Then "Lady Boothroyd of the Bypass" in inverted commas. Is beloved all right, William?

William Well, you can't put bonking, can you?

Sheila Do you like it?

William If that's what you want.

Sheila You've got to live with it, not me.

William Well, if it doesn't look right I'll let the grass grow. Where the devil are the others? Hubert's got to read the lesson.

Sheila (*looking at her watch*) Don't fuss, dear, it's only twenty to.

William I like that friend of Sally's.

Sheila Simon? So do I.

William I wonder if he's read my diaries yet?

Sheila Yes, I expect so, dear.

William He took them up to bed with him.

Sheila Well then, I'm sure he has.

William I must say Mousie gets on damned well with the budgerigar!

Hubert enters in a smart check suit, holding his pipe

Hubert The papers come yet, Mother?

Sheila Not yet.

William Where've you been? You'll be late for church.

Hubert Down to the stables. There's still twenty minutes.

William But you've got to read the lesson.

Hubert Yes, I know. What time do they arrive?

Sheila Soon, I expect.

William What is it? The new Bible?

Hubert (*sucking on his pipe*) No, the Vicar's doing that one. Mine is Judges. "The mother of Sisera looked out at a window and cried through the lattice: Why is his chariot so long in coming? Why tarry the wheels of his chariot?"

Sheila (*after a pause*) Is that all?

Hubert (*removing his pipe*) No, but that's the best bit.

William Well, why did they?

Hubert Sorry, Dad . . .

William Why did they tarry?
Hubert Tarry? I don't get you.
Sheila Sisera's wheels, dear.
Hubert I'm damned if I know.
Sheila But you must have read it, Hubert.
Hubert Yes, I have. But I've forgotten.
Sheila He's forgotten, dear.
William I've got it—I remember . . .
Hubert Well done, Father.
William Jael . . .
Hubert That's right, Jael—wife of Heber.
William What's that?
Hubert Heber, Father.
William Heber-Percy, do you mean?
Hubert No, Father.
William He commanded my brigade in India.
Hubert No, not him, Father.
William Why the devil bring him up, then?
Hubert I said Heber, Father—not Heber-Percy.
William No, not Percy. Walter was his name—not Percy.
Sheila I remember him—yes. Walter Heber-Percy, with a little black
    moustache.
William And Poodles.
Sheila That's right, dear.
William (*to Hubert*) He's not your fellow?
Hubert I don't think so, Father—dates don't fit too well.
William No, that's what I was thinking. How did we get on to him?
Sheila The lesson, dear.
William Yes, that's right. Well, why did they tarry?
Hubert Are you coming to church, Father?
William Yes.
Hubert Well, you'll find out, won't you? We'll all find out.
Sheila What fun you're going to have.
William A fellow read the lesson once, in India . . .
Sheila Oh, yes, dear . . .
William Heber-Percy's brigade major, actually—drank like a fish.
Sheila Oh, yes, dear?
William He got blotto in the mess the night before, and had this dreadful
    hangover. He went up to the lectern pretty goggily, and got hold of the
    old brass eagle by each wing, and shouted out: "And Moses said"—just
    like that, then he paused, and then—do you know what he said?
Hubert No, Father.
William Well, I'll tell you. He said it again: "And Moses said . . ."
Hubert (*chuckling*) Good heavens!
William I've not finished yet. "And Moses said"—and then he fixed the
    congregation with a bleary eye and said: "When this damned bird stops
    flapping its wings, I'll tell you what he said." What were we talking
    about?

Sheila (*hastily*) Never mind, dear. It's all over now. Hubert, what do you think of this? (*She takes out the card*)

Hubert What, Mother?

Sheila The inscription for my tombstone. (*She hands Hubert the card*)

William picks up his book and goes to the bookshelves again. Sheila throws him a look as he passes her. During the following he finds a book more to his liking and exchanges it for the one in his hand

Hubert Have you given this to anyone?

Sheila No not yet.

Hubert (*handing back the card*) Thank God!

Sheila Oh, I'm going to at eleven. I did think of adding, "Much loved Mother of Hubert Boothroyd, M.P.", but it came out quite expensive, so I thought I'd leave a space and you could add it in the future, if you ever felt that way, or if the Government put up your salary again.

Hubert Who are you seeing at eleven, Mother?

Sheila He's the husband of the sister of the man who made the greenhouse.

Hubert Saunderson.

William No—(*turning from the bookshelves*)—that's what I said, but she says "no".

Sheila Saunderson's the man who made the greenhouse, William. This man is his sister's husband.

William Not allowed.

Sheila What's not allowed?

William Deceased wife's sister—yes, but sister, no.

Sheila She's not his sister.

William Why the devil say she was, then?

Sheila I said she was Mr Saunderson's, not his. She's his wife.

William Whose?

Sheila Whatever he's called. He's a mason. (*To Hubert*) You must know him, Hubert.

William Wear's an apron, does he?

Sheila I don't know. I haven't met him yet.

William A lot of them do.

Sheila Well, of course. I'm not surprised, with all those chips.

William What chips?

Sheila Well, bits of granite. I expect it saves their suits.

William I've heard they do a lot of queer things, but I've never heard that they chip granite.

Hubert Father's talking about Masons—with a big M, Mother.

Sheila I'm afraid so, yes. Do tell him. I can't go on shouting.

William Do things with their fingers, like old Winston used to, only not so rude. I met one once, in Wolverhampton. He got tight. He told me lots of things, but not a word about the granite chipping. Still, that was some years ago, between the wars—I'll tell you when exactly—nineteen-twelve. The year they brought the King's horse down at Epsom.

Sheila That was not between the wars, dear.

William It depends which wars you mean. I went there to back the damned thing, in June when I was at Sandhurst. What was it called?

Sheila Does it matter?

William No—no—nothing like that. Herbert Tree was riding it. No, no, that can't be right. He was an actor fellow. Much too heavy.

Hubert Herbert Jones, Papa.

William That's it. Well done, my boy. Yes, Herbert Jones. Well, this daft suffragette ran out and brought it down. I'd had a pony on it, too, so I went up to Wolverhampton next time it came out, and met this Mason fellow.

Hubert Mother didn't mean that sort of Mason, Father.

William How the devil does she know what sort he was? She never met him. Anyway, they're all alike. They don't look any different from the rest of us, when they're in mufti.

Sheila William!

William Yes, dear?

Sheila If you don't stop talking about Masons, I'll scream.

William You started it, dear.

Hubert Mother meant the other kind of mason, Father, you know. (*He picks up the scissors from the sofa table and demonstrates by hitting the bowl of crocus with his pipe and scissors, and breaking it. A wedge of china falls out, and the peat spills*)

Sheila Hubert!

Hubert Sorry, Mother.

Sheila That's all right. It's always been cracked. (*She picks up the pieces of china*)

William What was the idea of doing that?

Sheila It was an accident, dear.

William Didn't look that way to me. What was the idea, Hubert?

Hubert I was demonstrating a stone-mason chipping stone.

William Why, suddenly? I've never seen a fellow do a thing like that before, have you, Sheila?

Sheila No, dear.

William What made you do it, Hubert? Most extraordinary!

Sheila Don't answer, Hubert. (*She rings for Robertson*)

William Ah! I get you! Jael!

Hubert Jael?

William She did that to Sisera. It all comes back now. With a tent peg and a hammer. That's what made him tarry.

Sheila That's right, William.

William Damn good demonstration. First class. Brought it all back. Wouldn't have remembered if you hadn't. Well done, Hubert, my boy.

Hubert Thank you, Father.

Robertson comes in

Robertson You rang, my lady?

Sheila Could you clear this, Robertson? There's been a little accident.

Robertson Yes, very good, my lady. (*He clears up the china and folds the peat into the table runner*)
Sheila Have the papers come yet?
Robertson No, not yet, my lady.

Maud comes in wearing her hat and with her handbag over her arm. She carries gloves and a Prayer Book, at which she is looking

William God bless my soul, the church flowers won't get much of a look-in this morning.

Maud ignores this. Robertson finishes clearing up the mess and folds over the runner

Sheila (*to Maud; explaining*) We've had a little accident.
Maud Oh, dear . . .

Robertson goes out with the runner

Hubert I broke a pot.
William Well worth it, if you ask me. He was demonstrating Jael killing Sisera.
Sheila They're in the Bible, dear. (*She puts the bowl of primroses on the sofa table*)
William Do it again, my boy.
Sheila (*snatching up the primroses*) No, William. Once is quite enough. (*She puts the primroses on the desk*)
Hubert Is Sally up yet?
Maud I've just woken her.
Hubert She'll be late.
Sheila Never mind. It's such a lovely day! And she can drive me to the village. (*She picks up the envelope and inscription, holding the envelope in front of the inscription so that Maud cannot see*) I've got an appointment with the mason at eleven. (*She puts her hand over her mouth*)
Hubert The stone-mason, Mother.
Sheila That's right, dear—yes. (*Emphatically*) The stone-mason.
William Maudie, ever met one?
Maud I don't know, off hand.
William I've just been telling them—I met one once, in Wolverhampton— what year was it, Hubert?

Sheila screams

What's the matter, dear? Has Mousie got out?
Sheila I said I'd scream if you went on about that beastly Mason.
William But . . .
Sheila William, don't argue, or I'll scream again. (*To Maud, holding out the inscription*) What do you think of this?

Maud reacts and sits down quickly on the sofa, putting the card on the sofa table. William sits turned away with his head bowed

Hubert Mother, Maud's allergic to that kind of joke—you ought to know that by now.
Sheila For the thousandth time, it's not a joke. I'm on my way to see the . . .
Hubert (*interrupting*) Mother!
Sheila Thank you, Hubert. The designer, at eleven.
Maud You can't let her, Hubert.

Robertson enters with the newspapers and puts them on the sofa table

Hubert I can't stop her. All I hope is that he'll think he's dealing with a harmless lunatic.
Sheila That's not very polite.
Hubert I'm sorry, Mother, but that's all one can hope. Otherwise he might start talking——

Sheila, spotting the headline on the top paper, puts on her spectacles

—if he took you at your word, and then the fat'll be in the fire.
Sheila It rather looks as if it's in the fire already, Hubert. (*Reading a headline from the "Sunday Express"*) "Lady Boothroyd of the Bypass——

Robertson moves to the half-open door, where he hovers

—Over my dead body, says her Ladyship . . ."

Hubert snatches the paper

Don't snatch, dear. (*To Maud*) Which would you like, Maud, *The Times* or the *Observer*?
Maud Neither, thank you, Sheila.
Sheila Don't be silly, dear. It's not the only item. (*She hands "The Sunday Times" to Maud*)

Hubert notices Robertson hovering, glares and moves towards the door, forcing Robertson to go

Robertson exits, closing the doors

There you are, dear. (*She picks up the "News of the World" and goes to William*) Which do you want, William? The *Observer* or the *News of the World*?
William Don't be daft, dear. (*He takes the "News of the World"*)
Hubert (*reading*) This is utterly disgraceful, Mother.
Sheila But you can't help reading it, dear. (*Sitting down*) Now let's see what the *Observer* has to say.

There is a short silence as everyone reads the papers, broken by Maud who lowers hers

Maud I just can't bear it, Hubert. I can't bear it.
Sheila Don't be so Victorian, dear. There are usually far worse things on

a Sunday. Hurry up and read it, then we'll swop. (*After a pause*) I can't
find anything in the *Observer*.
Hubert How did they get hold of it?
Sheila They evidently haven't. That's what worries me.
Hubert No—the *Express*, I mean.
Sheila (*still searching the "Observer"*) Oh, they'll get hold of anything, my
dear. They're a sort of printed flypaper!
Maud Oh, it's too awful.
Sheila Quite. (*Putting down the "Observer"*) It's either plain incompetence
or left-wing prejudice. (*To William*) There anything in yours, dear?
William Yes, a lot. Why is it always rectors?
Hubert Where's the *Sunday Telegraph*?
Sheila It should be here.
Hubert You finished, Maud?
Maud Yes.
Hubert Right, then.

*Hubert and Maud swop. Hubert takes "The Times" from Maud, and gives
her the "Express"*

Sheila That's extremely selfish, Hubert.
William Anyone'd think that there was no-one in the country but a lot
of crazy rectors in shorts. Listen to this . . .
Sheila We'd rather not, dear.
William Well, you're missing something. Good, the bishop's torn him off
a strip. Quite right. It's discipline the church wants. All this turn-the-
other-cheek stuff doesn't work. (*To Hubert*) What's wrong with you, my
boy?
Hubert I don't think that I've ever been quite so disgusted, Father.
William Oh, it's in *The Sunday Times* too, is it? By Jove, they are coming
on! (*He takes "The Sunday Times" from Hubert*) I'll bet it doesn't quote
the organist in full, though, does it?
Hubert How did they get hold of it?

Simon enters unnoticed, with the "Sunday Telegraph" in his hand

Sheila Don't ask me, dear.
Hubert I am asking you.
Sheila Good heavens! You're an M.P., Hubert—you should know the
Press get hold of anything and everything. They have their sources.
William Nothing here except a lot of blah about some daft old woman
who—my goodness, it's you, my dear! What have you been up to? Oh,
lord, it's the bypass again!
Maud Here's a photograph.
Hubert What?
Maud Yes, look. (*Reading captions*) "Lady Boothroyd, at the graveside."
Hubert Who took that?
Maud It says here—"Photographed by Simon Green".
Hubert You mean to say you let him take that, Mother?

Sheila Well, he had a camera. And he's a guest, and it's so rude, I always think, if someone wants . . .

Simon drifts into the room with a folded "Sunday Telegraph" in his hand

Simon Good morning.
Sheila Good morning, dear.
Hubert Are you responsible for this, young man?
Simon What?
Hubert You know damn well what.
Sheila Look, Simon. (*She takes the paper from Hubert and shows it to Simon*)
Hubert You should be ashamed of yourself, young man.
Maud Yes, how could you!
Simon It's my job—that's how.
Hubert Your job! To get a daft old woman in your lens, and make a fool of her!
Sheila Hubert, if you're going to talk like that, you'd better leave the room.
Hubert I'm sorry, Mother—but it makes me see red.
Simon And apart from being my job, I thought that your mother ought to have the chance to sway public opinion . . .
Sheila Quite right!
Simon And not just be snuffed out, like a candle.
William Not bad. That should make 'em sit up. I wonder who wrote it?
Simon I did.
William Well done.
Hubert (*outraged*) Well done, Father!
Sheila Make who sit up, William?
William Fellows in Whitehall, of course.
Sheila You really think so?
William 'Course I do. You can't have hari-kari every time you want to make a bypass. There's enough of it when it's been made, good heavens!
Sheila Hubert, ring the Minister of Transport.
Hubert I don't know his number.
Sheila Put a personal call through to Transport House, then.

The church bells start

Hubert Transport House is not the Ministry of Transport, Mother.
Sheila Well, it should be.
Maud Go on, Hubert. There's the bells! You must do something or you'll be late for church.
Hubert Oh lord! (*He goes to the telephone*)
Sheila That's right, dear. (*To Maud*) I knew you'd see sense. I'll ring for Robertson. He takes the *Sunday Mirror*. (*She goes to ring the bell*)
William Did you read my diaries, my boy?
Simon Well, I've started on them, sir.
William Where have you got to?
Simon Lloyd George—when he came out to France.

Sheila Oh, that reminds me—Simon's got a song, dear, about Mr Lloyd George. You'd love it.
Hubert (*holding the receiver*) Be quiet, Mother. I can't hear.
Sheila Oh—sorry, dear.

Robertson enters

Robertson You rang, my lady?
Hubert Quiet, man! (*Into the phone*) Come on, come on . . .
Sheila (*whispering*) Have you got the *Sunday Mirror*, Robertson, please?
Robertson Yes, my lady.
Sheila Is there anything about me in it?
Robertson Is there not, my lady. Plastered right across the middle page.
William Plastered? Who's plastered?
Hubert Be quiet, Father. (*Into the phone*) Hullo, operator, I'd like a personal call to the Minister of Transport, Ministry of Transport, London . . . I don't know, I haven't got a London book.
William Who's plastered?
Sheila Sssh!
Hubert It's Hubert Boothroyd, M.P. . . . Two-five-oh . . . Yes, in the next three minutes, if you don't mind, as I have to go to church to read the lesson. And if he's not there, I'd like to know where he is. (*He hangs up and looks at Sheila*)
Sheila (*to William*) Go and get your hat and coat on, William, if you're going to go to church. And give the Vicar my love.
William Right. Where's my book?
Sheila In your hand.
William Ah, yes. (*Trying again*) When did you get plastered, Sheila?
Sheila Oh dear. Robertson just meant there was a picture of me in the *Sunday Mirror*—plastered right across the middle page. The picture—not me.
William Oh, yes. I was going to say I haven't seen you plastered since Armistice Night.

William exits

Hubert (*jigging the phone*) Come on—come on . . .

Robertson enters with the "Sunday Mirror" and the "People". He gives the "Mirror" to Sheila. The church bells stop

Maud Leave it alone, dear.
Sheila Thank you, Robertson.
Maud Hubert!
Hubert Yes?
Maud What about the Vicar?
Hubert What about him?
Sheila Isn't that good?

Sheila sits and Simon squats beside her

Do look, Maud.

Maud I'll be late for church. Sheila, shall I ask the Vicar to supper tonight?

Sheila Yes, do, dear. He's so nice.

Maud You must come, Hubert, now.

Hubert I can't.

Maud But what about the lesson?

Hubert You'll have to read it!

Maud Oh, no!

Maud goes

Sheila Thank you so much, Robertson.

Robertson Thank you, my lady. Would you like to see the *People*?

Sheila The people? What people?

Robertson hands her the newspaper

(*Comprehending*) Oh, the *People*. (*She sees the photograph*)

Sally enters

Sally Have the Sundays come yet, Robertson?

Robertson Indeed they have, miss.

Robertson goes, with the "Mirror"

Sheila Sally, Simon's taken such a clever photograph—look.

Sally (*peering over Sheila's shoulder*) Oh, that's marvellous.

The telephone rings. Hubert picks up the receiver

There any more?

Simon Yes, here—look. (*He shows Sally the "Sunday Telegraph"*)

Hubert (*to them*) *Quiet!* (*Into the phone*) Hullo . . . Yes, Hubert Boothroyd speaking . . . Boothroyd, M.P. Could I speak to the Minister, please?

Sally Oh, what a super picture!

Hubert Sssh!

Sheila Hush, dear.

Hubert (*into the phone*) When will he be back? . . . For a late supper? . . . Oh, is he? I see. Thanks. (*He hangs up*) He's sailing up the Solent with a friend.

A single bell tolls

Sally (*to Hubert*) You haven't said good morning, Daddy.

Hubert I don't feel inclined to.

Sheila Good luck with the chariot wheels, dear.

Hubert exits

Sally He won't ever forgive you, darling.
Simon Never mind. It isn't him I'm marrying.
Sheila Quite right.

The telephone rings. The single bell stops. Simon goes to the phone

(*To Simon*) Thank you, Simon.
Simon (*lifting the receiver*) Hullo? . . . Yes, she is . . . Who's speaking?
. . . Hold on. Lady Boothroyd, it's for you.
Sheila Who is it?
Simon *Panorama.*
Sheila Oh, how too exciting! (*She goes to the telephone*) Hullo? . . . Yes,
it is . . . Yes, so have I . . . Oh, how nice. Which do you like best? . . .
The one beside the grave. Oh, I'm so glad. It's such a clever photograph.
My future grandson took it. Well, grandson-in-law, I should say . . .
When? . . . Today? . . . Would you come here or would I have to come
to you? . . . How very nice of you. Well, any time that suits you . . .
About four. Yes, perfect. We'll expect you when we see you . . . Thank
you so much. Good-bye. (*She hangs up*) They're going to make a record
of me.
Sally Grannie—you on *Panorama*—you'll be famous!
Sheila I suppose I will, dear. Oh well, better late than never. (*She picks up
the inscription*) Will you drive me to the village, dear?
Sally Yes, O.K., Grannie. What time?
Sheila Just as soon as you're ready.
Sally It's a pity that you won't be seeing *Panorama*, isn't it?

Sheila Perhaps I will, dear. Perhaps I'll be passing Telstar.

William enters

William Sheila! Sheila!
Sheila William, you aren't still here?
William I've no cash for the collection.

*Sheila goes to her bag on the sofa. The telephone rings. Simon goes to answer
it*

Simon (*on the phone*) Hullo? . . . Yes, he is. (*To William*) For you, sir.
William Probably old Gerald.
Sheila You'll be late, William. (*She takes out a one-pound note and a fifty-
pence piece*)
William Never mind. I know the old *Venite* off by heart. (*He takes the
phone*) Gerald? . . . William here. I'm late for church . . . You've seen
the papers, have you? . . . Then you know my problem . . . Yes, I think
that's right. Around one . . . Good . . . Good-bye. (*He hangs up*) He's
only going to lay for one.

*William moves across the room, followed by Sheila with the collection money
from her bag, as—*

the CURTAIN *falls*

ACT II

SCENE 1

The same. Sunday evening, after dinner

Sheila, Maud and Sally are having coffee, waiting for the men to come out of the dining-room. Sheila is dozing. Maud refills Sheila's coffee-cup, which is beginning to tilt a little precariously

Sheila (*opening her eyes*) Thank you, dear. What nice young men those *Panorama* people were, and so hard-working. I feel quite exhausted.

Sally Why not have a drink, then?

Sheila No, dear. I had quite a lot of wine at supper. Actually, I got on quite well with that funny-looking camera. I do hope that I said the right things.

Maud Sheila, has the Vicar talked to you yet?

Sheila No, dear. He did try at supper, but I put him off. I switched him on to the fund for the church roof. He admitted that he'd overspent a little. So I promised I'd pay the overdraft off.

Sally How much, Grannie?

Sheila Seven thousand pounds.

Sally Good heavens!

Sheila Yes, it is a lot of money. But that's what he said he'd been praying for, and so I didn't want to disappoint him.

Maud I hoped he'd make you see sense, Sheila.

Sheila Well, he hasn't had much chance yet. And I think he settled for the seven thousand in the end with a clear conscience. And after all, I am doing him out of the burial fees. No, I mustn't talk like that on my last evening.

Sally Don't tell me they charge for burying you, Grannie?

Sheila But, of course, dear. How else do you think the clergy live? I should imagine that the burial fees add up to a very reasonable total. And, of course, it's an unending source of income.

Maud looks round to see if the others are coming

That's the beauty of it. (*Noticing Maud's look*) Really, William is a little selfish sitting in the dining-room so long on my last evening. Robertson's the only one who's taken any trouble. William seems to think it's just like any other Sunday evening. Well—I think I'll go and get my packing done.

Maud Your packing!

Sheila Putting away, I mean. Maud, do try to cheer up, or you'll spoil the party.

Maud I can't, Sheila. (*She gets out her handkerchief*)

Sally Mother!

Sheila Nonsense, dear, if I can put a good face on it, so can you. I'm going to leave you these. (*She shows Maud her necklace*)

Maud (*upset*) No, Sheila, I can't bear it.

Sheila Rubbish, dear. You've always known they'd be yours. You'll find them in the jewel-box on the dressing-table in the morning. (*Indicating her bracelet*) I'm leaving you this, Sally.

Sally Grannie, you can't!

Sheila Well, it won't be any use to me, dear, will it?

Sally Oh, it's lovely . . .

Sheila You can always pop it, dear.

Sally I never will. I've always loved it.

Maud Sally!

Sally Well, we might as well be honest, Mummy. I can't bear all this hypocrisy about death, can you, Grannie?

Sheila No, I quite agree, dear. Talk about an ill wind blowing somebody good!

Maud This'll ruin Hubert.

Sheila On the contrary, it'll make him. He's come out of it extremely well today. A man who sticks up for his mother's bound to be a vote-catcher.

Maud (*sobbing*) He says he'll cut off Sally if she marries Simon.

Sheila Yes, I've been expecting that. So I've decided to leave all the money I was going to leave to him, to Sally.

Sally (*with a shriek*) Grannie!

Maud Oh, dear!

Sheila Then she can support that nice young man of hers when he runs out of scoops.

William enters, followed by Hubert and the Vicar

William The master lost the hounds—they were the bitch pack, Vicar— that's important to remember.

Vicar Yes, Sir William.

William Well, he rode up to a yokel leaning on a gate and shouted: "Have you seen the hounds?" "Aye, sir", the yokel shouted back. "Hounds went past here ten minutes back." "And did you see the fox?" the master shouted. "Aye, sir", shouted back the yokel. "Fox were lying third or fourth and going well."

Vicar Why was the fox so far behind, Sir William?

William It had rheumatism, Vicar.

Vicar Ah, I see. And yet, in spite of that, it took part in the chase. What an inspiring story.

Sheila (*rising*) Well, I think I'll go and pack.

The men turn to look at her

I won't be long.

Sally I'll come and help you, Grannie.

Sheila Thank you, dear. That's very kind of you.

Sheila and Sally go out

William Pack? Who does she think she is—Tutankhamen?

Hubert Vicar, you will talk to her, won't you, when she comes back?

Vicar Yes, of course I will, but do you really think she means to go through with it?

Hubert Yes, I do. When Mother digs her heels in, it's quite something Well, Maud knows that, don't you?   ·

Vicar So she's threatened this before?

Maud pours coffee for the men

Maud Oh, no—she can be very obstinate, but nothing like this.

Vicar Like what, for example?

William Well, she pestered Winston in the war about the toilet paper shortage in the village. Wrote him seven letters, till she got an answer.

Vicar And I'm sure it was worth reading.

William Three-ton lorries, seven of them, packed up to the canvas. I doubt if they're through it yet. You weren't here then, were you, Padre?

Vicar No, no—I was serving in a frigate.

William What's that?

Vicar (*much louder*) Frigate!

William What did he say, Hubert?

Hubert He was serving in a frigate, Father.

William My mistake.

Maud I'm sure that you could help my mother-in-law, Vicar.

Vicar Well, I'll do my best.

Maud If you could only speak to her and make her see how wicked it is. It is wicked, isn't it?

Vicar Oh, yes, indeed.

Maud She doesn't seem to see that. She seems quite—well, quite ethereal, somehow.

William She's bonking, that's what's wrong with her—mad as a March hare. Always has been—always will be—not surprising, really, if you ever saw her father. Thought he was a camel!

Vicar Really?

William Don't believe me, do you?

Vicar Yes, Sir William—if you say so.

William Well, I'm saying so. He thought he was a camel.

Vicar Yes, indeed.

Maud You never told me, Hubert.

William Don't worry, my dear. He wasn't one! You never met him, did you, Hubert? Died before you turned up, didn't he?

Hubert I think so, Father.

William Died the year we married, in fact. When was that?

Hubert In nineteen-twenty-two, Papa.

William That's right, yes. April. I was fishing on the Oykell, and a fellow
ran down to the river with a message. Damned annoying, as the fish
were taking well. I had to go to Inverness and catch the night mail down
to Ipswich. (*To the Vicar*) He was Lord St Edwards.

Vicar Ah, yes.

William And he thought he was a camel.

Vicar So you said, Sir William.

William Used to drink a jug of water every morning after breakfast, and
then never touched another drop till breakfast the next day. What do
you think he died of? Water on the brain! Well, he was asking for it,
wasn't he?

Vicar Yes, I suppose so.

William But he didn't do too badly—ninety-four, he was, when he conked
out. Quite harmless. Charming fellow. In the Tenth Hussars. But harmless. Then he was a Liberal M.P. till he succeeded. Then the trouble
started. Did I tell you that he thought he was a camel?

Vicar Yes, Sir William.

William Well, I'm wrong. He didn't. My mind must be going. Dromedary
not a camel! That's the two-humped fellow, isn't it?

Vicar So I believe, Sir William.

William That's right. Shoulder-blades, you see. That's how he got the
idea. He had two, whereas a camel's only got one. So it must have been
a dromedary. How did we get on to him?

Hubert Through Mother, Father.

William Ah, yes. People tried to stop us marrying. Would have, in fact,
except that my side was as sound as a bell. And it didn't turn out badly.
Never thought you were a dromedary, have you, Hubert?

Hubert Not yet, Father, no.

William And I'll bet you've never drunk a jug of water after breakfast, or
at any other time, eh, Vicar?

Simon enters with the diaries. Hubert sees him and moves away

There you are, my boy! Now tell me, where've you got to?

Simon Nineteen-forty-three. The Home Guard.

William Have you got to the time Robertson got tight and stopped the
district nurse and said she was a parachutist?

Simon No, sir, not yet.

William Took her skirt off in the Institute to prove it. There was hell to
pay. I had to give her brandy, and I'm damned if she'd put it on again.

Maud Vicar, I'm sure it'll be better if you talk to her alone.

Vicar Yes, I agree.

Hubert Well, when she comes back, we'll leave you. All right, Father?

William What's that?

Hubert We'll leave the Vicar here alone to talk to Mother.

William What's that?

Hubert Her threat, of course.

William It won't do any damned good—I've been talking to her now for fifty years—and where's it got me? She's as obstinate as hell. Let's have a drink.

Hubert I'll ring for Robertson. (*He rings the bell*)

William Thanks, Hubert. Gets it from her father, Lord St Edwards. I'll tell you something, Vicar.

Hubert You've already told him, Father.

William What? About the camel?

Hubert No, the dromedary.

William Oh, good. Quite extraordinary, eh, Vicar? Not as if the fellow didn't have a looking-glass.

Robertson enters with a tray of drinks

Robertson You rang, Sir William?

Hubert Drinks, please, Robertson. (*He turns and sees them*) Oh, well done.

Robertson places the drinks on a table and moves towards the door. Simon sits at the piano

William Vicar, did you see the way that bishop in the *News of the World* chewed that rector up?

Vicar No—we don't take that paper.

William Pity. Robertson ! . . .

Robertson Sir William?

William Where's the *News of the World*, man? I bet you've got it.

Robertson Very good, Sir William.

Robertson goes

William Why is it some rectors are called vicars, and some vicars rectors, Vicar?

Vicar It's the rector has the living.

William It's the rector does the living, if you ask me! (*He is very amused by this*) You're a vicar, aren't you?

Vicar Yes, indeed.

William Well, take my tip and stick to it. (*He goes to Simon at the piano*) Hello, you going to sing us something?

Robertson enters with the "News of the World"

Robertson The *News of the World*, Sir William.

William Thank you. Now then, listen to this . . .

Robertson exits

Hubert I'm quite sure the Vicar doesn't want to hear that, Father.

William Don't you?

Vicar Well, I think I'd rather have a glass of whisky.

William Good idea. Well, take it home and read it, if you feel like it,

(He gives the paper to the Vicar)
Vicar Thank you.
William Not a bit. I've read it.
Hubert Whisky, Father?
William Why not?
Hubert You, Maud?
Maud Yes, I think I will, tonight.

Hubert pours and distributes whiskies

Sheila enters

Sheila (*to Simon*) Ah, there you are. Give Sally a hand with my suitcase, will you, there's an angel.

Simon goes out

Please don't get up, Vicar. I am so sorry that I didn't come to church this morning. I was choosing coffins. Did they tell you? And I got one off the peg. I was too lucky! They'd had an overlapping order—duplicated on the telephone, or something. It was just exactly what I wanted, and—(*to William*)—I put it down to you, dear. I do hope you don't mind, but I hadn't got my cheque-book with me. I think I'll have a whisky, Hubert. I feel so elated. Everybody's being so nice to me. Mr Saunderson's relation's sweet, and he says he can do the headstone. And do you know what those two sweet children did this afternoon? They tidied up the grave. I didn't think you'd want me in the graveyard, Vicar, so I thought I'd make my own arrangements.

Hubert hands Sheila a drink

Thank you, Hubert. Have you rung the Minister of Transport?
Hubert I tried once. He was engaged.
Sheila I'm very glad to hear it. That should mean he's got the wind up, shouldn't it? Well, did I miss a lot this morning? Tell me, somebody. How was the sermon, William? Very dull? Oh, I'm so sorry, Vicar— I've got so much on my mind. Have some more whisky.
Vicar Well, perhaps a soupçon.
Sheila Hubert, give the Vicar some more whisky.

Hubert does so

William Vicar—ever hear the story of the minister in Scotland who was boring them stiff with his sermon?
Vicar I don't think so.
William Well, they have these galleries up there, for local big-wigs, in some kirks, like a box in a theatre, behind a lot of panelling and half-way to the ceiling—out of sight, to all intents and purposes. You get me?
Vicar Yes, Sir William.
William Well, the minister was boring on, as I say, and he paused just

before his peroration, just for a split second, and the laird's voice rang
out loud and clear—guess what it said?

Vicar I can't, Sir William.

William Well, I'll tell you—it said: "Three no-trumps."

The telephone rings

Sheila Hubert, it's sure to be for you.

Hubert picks up the receiver

Hubert (*into the phone*) Hullo? . . . Yes, thank you, speaking . . . Oh,
hullo, sir . . . Yes, I did, but they said you were sailing . . . Oh, I see.
And what did the P.M. say? . . . Well, that could be true, but it's not
going to stop her . . . No, she's adamant . . . Of course she isn't bluffing.
She's already had her grave dug, as you know. And she's just bought a
coffin, in the village, and a tombstone, and she's had an interview this
afternoon with *Panorama*. You must do something! . . . But damn it
all, man, she's my mother! . . . Well, of course, it makes a difference.
Put yourself in my shoes. How would you feel if your mother . . . What's
that? . . . Oh, I'm sorry. But mine isn't. She's still very much alive, sir,
and she won't be in the morning, unless you do something . . . Yes, at
eight o'clock, as soon as the bulldozers come. With great respect, sir,
you could ring the P.M. up again and tell him that she isn't bluffing, and
that it'll look bad for him if she goes through with it . . . You will? Right.
Thanks very much, sir. Good-bye. (*He rings off*) Well, he's going to
ring the P.M. once again, and then call me back.

Sheila What did he say the P.M. said when he first spoke to him?

Hubert That he's heard you weren't all there.

William He's damned well informed. You've got to hand it to him.

Hubert Well, it's up to you now, Vicar. Come along, Maud, what about
a game of billiards?

Sheila Billiards?

Maud Oh, I'd love that.

Hubert Come on, Father, you can mark.

William Mark what?

Hubert For us at billiards.

William What's the point—you never score.

Hubert The Vicar wants to talk to Mother, Father.

William I'm not stopping him.

Sheila Of course you aren't, dear.

William No use talking to her, anyway. I've tried for years.

Hubert and Maud go, Hubert closing the door

She's all yours, Vicar.

Sheila William, you're too embarrassing.

William Give him another glass of whisky.

Sheila What a good idea. I'm sure it'll relax you. (*She takes the Vicar's
glass to the table*)

William Top me up too, will you, dear?

Sheila refills the glasses and hands them out

Vicar The news this morning gave us all a great shock in the village, Lady Boothroyd. It gave my wife quite a turn at breakfast. And then, when she passed the paper to me, I was stricken speechless for a moment. I could scarcely believe my eyes.

Sheila hands him his glass

Er—thank you. And at Matins, everybody was dumbfounded, as Sir William no doubt noticed.
William What's that?
Sheila Matins, dear. They were dumbfounded.
William I don't blame them! Where the devil did she get it from?
Vicar I don't think I quite follow you, Sir William.
William Maud's hat. That's what you're on to, isn't it?
Sheila No, dear. The Vicar means the news about me.
William Oh, that! Couldn't say—I didn't notice. Everybody looked about as glum as usual. Something wrong with Matins, if you ask me, Vicar.
Vicar Oh, I'm sorry you think that.
Sheila I think I'll miss it least of everything—except the ordering. I wonder if God feels as bored as the greengrocer must, to hear the same old list each week. Oh well, perhaps I'll have a chance to ask him.

William shuts his eyes, apparently dozing

Vicar You're bluffing, Lady Boothroyd. Tell me you're bluffing.
Sheila No, indeed I'm not.
Vicar You really mean to go through with it?
Sheila Yes, of course I do.
Vicar You mustn't, Lady Boothroyd, I beseech you. It's a sin to take your own life.
Sheila Well, it may be, but it's not as bad as taking other people's—and that's going on the whole time. Well, just look at William. He's been doing it for years, and been paid for it. Ordering men into battle, to lay down their lives without the least idea what they were doing it for. It was just the same with you when you were in the Navy. You saw nothing wrong in preaching to the sailors and telling them they were dying for a cause. My cause is different, that's all. And I'm not involving anyone else.
Vicar I really don't know what to say.
Sheila Of course you don't. You haven't got a leg to stand on. Tell me about Heaven, Vicar. Is it really like you say it is?
Vicar I haven't any doubt at all.
Sheila (*slightly tiddly*) Those pearly gates, and harps. How too exciting! Just think, I'll see it tomorrow morning. Or do you suppose the journey takes a long time?
Vicar I'm afraid I couldn't tell you . . .
Sheila Well, of course not, we're all guessing, aren't we? I will get in,

won't I, Vicar—I've been very good.

Vicar I'm sure you have.

Sheila I've never looked at anyone but William. I'll get good marks for that, surely? (*To William*) Well, you haven't been as easy as you might have been, dear.

William (*opening his eyes*) What about Tim Carson?

Sheila What about him?

William Well, you looked at him, all right.

Sheila Oh, well, yes. But he was good-looking. (*To the Vicar*) Tim was William's second-in-command, a real Adonis, with the bluest eyes you ever saw. We used to play golf at North Berwick, when the regiment was waiting to go overseas. And I'm afraid we didn't always finish the round. But he was good-looking.

William What about the night you had to stay in an hotel in Edinburgh, because of the fog?

Sheila Well, we stayed there.

William There was no fog at North Berwick.

Sheila So you always told me, dear. Well, we must have been lucky—I mean you must—oh dear, I've had too much whisky. Dear Tim, do you think I'll find him there tomorrow?

William Tim! Depends if any hotel managers have got there first. Talking of Maud's hat, Vicar . . .

Vicar Maud's hat?

William Yes, in church this morning.

Vicar Ah, yes . . .

William It reminded me of Lady Salisbury. Not this one—or the one before—the one before that. Did you ever hear what happened to her?

Vicar No, I think not.

William Well, she had a wedding and a funeral to go to the same after-noon in Hatfield. You know, stillroom maid and footman, and one of the coachman's widows—usual week-end turnover. Well, as the funeral took place first, at two, and the wedding second, at two-thirty, she decided she'd park her wedding hat in the porch. Get me?

Vicar Yes, Sir William.

William Well, when she came down the aisle after the funeral, it wasn't there. And it was only when she got out in the open that she spotted it. Do you know where it was?

Vicar I've no idea, Sir William.

William On the coffin with the other floral tributes. Still, she nabbed it just as they were going to plant it.

The telephone rings. As neither Sheila nor William makes any move to answer it, the Vicar rises to pick up the receiver

Vicar Hullo? . . . Yes, it is. Hold on. I'll get him.

Hubert and Maud enter

(*To Hubert*) It's for you.

Hubert takes the receiver

Hubert (*into the phone*) Hullo?... Yes, speaking... Yes, I see. And what did the P.M. say?... I see. And that's final?... Oh well, thank you anyway for trying. Good-bye. (*He replaces the receiver*) Nothing doing, Mother.

Sheila Do you mean they won't give in?

Hubert No. He said that the P.M.'s adamant.

Sheila Oh, is he? Well then, so am I.

Hubert I told him that the first time.

Sheila Well, I wasn't, then. I could have been persuaded. But not now. I'm in dead earnest. I'm so sorry, everybody, but I'm really angry. (*Angrily*) Oh!

Hubert It's no use flying off the handle, Mother.

Sheila It's too late—I've flown. Forgive me, Vicar, I'll calm down in a minute.

Vicar I feel that I really should be going, Lady Boothroyd.

Sheila Not yet. Why don't we sing "Lloyd George knew my father"?

William What the devil's that?

Sheila A song that Simon taught me. Oh, I'm so glad I remembered. (*Calling*) Simon! Simon! (*To William*) You'll love it, William. And it's my last chance to teach you.

Simon enters, followed by Sally

Simon, come along. We're going to all sing "Lloyd George knew my father".

Vicar But I really should be going, Lady Boothroyd.

Sheila Must you?

Vicar Yes. I think my wife will soon be worrying.

Sheila Well, stay and hear a verse or two, and then slip out without a word. I'd like you all to do that, actually. I hate "good-byes"—just slip out without saying anything. I'll go on playing to myself a little, and then go to bed. (*There is a pause while she looks at them all*) Now—tomorrow morning. (*To Hubert*) Breakfast's at seven-forty-five for you, dear, as you have a train to catch. The rest at nine, or when you feel like it.

William We'll all be down before eight, Sheila. Don't be daft.

Sheila Oh, will you? Well, that's very touching. All right. Seven-forty-five for everyone.

Hubert Including you, I hope.

Sheila No, dear, I won't be coming down. (*She turns to the piano*)

Vicar Could we not have another little talk, perhaps?

Sheila No, Vicar, there's no more to be said. (*To William*) Come along, dear. (*She takes William to the piano and seats herself*)

Everyone turns towards the piano

Now then, Simon, are you ready?

Simon O.K.

Sheila plays a chord

Sally Good-bye, Grannie.
Sheila Good-bye, darling. Oh, I said I wouldn't say that.

Sally hugs Sheila, then gives her a kiss

It's just what I wanted to avoid. But thank you, all the same. (*She disengages herself from Sally*) Now, Simon . . . (*She plays, and starts singing*)

Simon takes up singing "Lloyd George knew my father—my father knew Lloyd George". Hubert joins him, then William, then the rest of them. Soon it is too much for Maud, who breaks down and goes towards the door, followed by Hubert

Robertson enters, then holds the door open as in turn Maud, Hubert and the Vicar pass him to exit. Simon joins Sally and takes her hand, and they exit in their turn. As they go, they are all singing in a manner reminiscent of a choir and clergy going down the aisle in church

When the others have gone, Sheila and William go on singing. Robertson comes into the room. They still sing on, to his amazement. He tidies the dirty glasses and puts them on the tray. Sheila stops singing, but William goes on. She continues to play, softly

Sheila Be quiet, William.
William Sorry, my dear. (*He stops singing*)
Sheila Breakfast seven-forty-five, please, Robertson, for all except me.
Robertson Very good, my lady. Will you have yours upstairs?
Sheila No, I won't be having any, Robertson. Good night.
Robertson (*moving away*) Good night, my lady. (*Continuing*) And good-bye.

Robertson goes

Sheila starts playing loudly again, to drown the word, and plays much louder as he goes out. William joins her again and then moves away, singing still, turns round, looks at her, still singing, turns away

William goes out, singing still, but in a broken voice

Sheila sings on bravely "Onward, Christian Soldiers, Marching as to War . . .", reverting to the words of the song, as—

the CURTAIN *falls*

SCENE 2

The same. The following morning

When the CURTAIN *rises Robertson is discovered laying the breakfast table.
He straightens the cloth, then goes to look out of the window, and also looks
at his watch. He returns to the trolley, picks up a cup and saucer and is about
to put it in Sheila's place when he remembers she is not coming down to
breakfast, so he puts the cup noisily in Hubert's place. Sally enters in a suitably sober dress*

Robertson Good morning, miss.
Sally Is no-one down yet?
Robertson No, miss—not yet.

Sally looks at the food on the table without appetite

Any news, miss?
Sally How should I know? Her door's locked. I tried it on my way down.
Robertson So's the one out of Sir William's room into her ladyship's.
You think she'd say good-bye to him.
Sally (*picking up Sheila's knitting from the back of the sofa*) She hates
good-byes. She wouldn't even say them last night. (*She replaces the knit-
ting*)
Robertson That's right, miss. She started singing when I tried it. Daftest
song you ever heard, about some nob who knew her father.
Sally How was Grandpa when you called him?
Robertson Fast asleep, miss. Then when I put down his tea, he opened up
one eye and said: "There's something on this morning, Robertson. What
is it?" So I told him.
Sally What did he do then?
Robertson He sat up and told me what clothes to lay out for him, calm
as you please. You'd never think her ladyship was . . .
Sally I don't think death worries him a lot. He's seen too much of it.
Robertson But she's his wife, miss.
Sally I know. But so was his regiment. Well, you should know.
Robertson That's true, miss.
Sally That's what he's been trained for, all his life. To look death in the
face, and carry on—regardless.
Robertson But it's her who's looking in its face, not him, miss.
Sally Yes. But that's what he's been used to.
Robertson P'raps you're right, miss. P'raps that's why he's put me on to
sounding the "Last Post" at eight o'clock.
Sally No—you don't mean it!
Robertson I do mean it, miss, and no mistake. He wouldn't let me have
a bit of practice either, so as not to upset her. I haven't sounded it for
thirty years.

Robertson listens to a distant mechanized sound which starts up, then continues, with his head on one side

They're coming, miss.

Sally Who?

Robertson The bulldozers.

Sally goes to the window

Simon enters

Simon They're coming down the road.

Robertson That's right, sir.

Simon Can you see them yet?

Robertson Not yet, sir. They're half a mile away, behind the hill. (*He looks at his watch*) They're dead on time. They'll start at eight o'clock all right, and no mistake.

Robertson goes out

Simon goes to the trolley, pours himself a cup of coffee and holds up the jug

Simon What about some breakfast, darling?

Sally I'm not hungry.

Simon Oh, come on.

Sally I feel so awful, Simon. We encouraged her. I didn't think she'd ever do it.

Simon Nor did I. Come on, have something.

Sally No, I don't want anything.

Simon Well, I do, I'm afraid.

Sally How can you! I'm surprised that you're not hiding in her bedroom, with your camera.

Simon I thought of that. But the door was locked.

Sally Do you mean to say you tried it?

Simon Yes, I tried to speak to her. Darling, your grandfather was in the bath and he'd left his door open. There was a red coat hanging on a chair. You don't suppose he's going hunting, do you?

Sally Not unless he's gone mad.

Simon He's been mad for years.

Sally Don't talk like that.

Simon You haven't read his diaries.

Hubert enters in a dark suit and goes slowly towards the window

Sally 'Morning, Daddy.

Simon 'Morning, sir.

Hubert does not answer, but goes to get his egg from the trolley in silence, then sits in his place

Robertson enters with the toast, which he puts on the table

Simon stands looking out of the window

Robertson Good morning, sir.
Hubert Good morning, Robertson.
Robertson They're here, sir.
Hubert Yes, I know. I hear them.
Robertson They'll start on the dot.
Hubert Yes, I expect so.
Robertson Mr Hubert, I'm turned eighty, and I've not seen . . .
Hubert I know, Robertson.

Robertson goes

Sally Daddy—she hasn't . . .
Hubert Not that I'm aware of.
Sally Why the black tie, then?
Hubert I'm catching the eight-twenty, that's why.
Sally Daddy, go and talk to her, please.
Hubert How can I? Her door's locked.
Sally Well, talk through the keyhole. I did, but she didn't answer.
Hubert There you are, then. (*He bangs his egg with his spoon*)
Sally (*after a pause*) Daddy . . .
Hubert Yes? What is it now?
Sally She's leaving me the money she was going to leave you. Did she tell you?
Hubert What!
Sally She told me last night.

Maud enters, in a black dress

Hubert Maud, is this true?
Maud Is what true?
Simon 'Morning, Mrs Boothroyd.
Maud 'Morning, Simon. (*To Hubert*) Is what true, dear?
Sally About Grannie leaving me the money she was going to leave to Daddy.
Maud Well, that's what she told us last night.
Hubert Oh, damn!

Hubert rises, throws down his napkin, and goes out

Maud (*looking after him*) Where's he going?
Sally I expect he's going to plead with Grannie through the keyhole.
Maud She won't answer. I've been trying.
Sally Oh dear. You don't think that she's already . . . ?
Maud How should I know, dear?

The Vicar enters and comes slowly to Maud

Good morning, Vicar.
Vicar 'Morning, Mrs Boothroyd. 'Morning, Sally. 'Morning, Simon. Any
  —er . . . ?
Maud No, not yet.

The bulldozers are heard in the distance

Would you like some breakfast?
Vicar No, no. Where is Lady Boothroyd now?
Sally Up in her room.
Vicar Do you think that my presence, upstairs, now, would help?
Maud I doubt it, Vicar. Her door's locked. Unless you think that you can
  function from the landing.
Vicar Oh dear! And where is Sir William?
Simon He was in his bath just now.

There is an awkward pause, broken by the Vicar

Vicar (*after looking upwards*) May I say how becoming you look, Mrs
  Boothroyd.
Maud Thank you, Vicar. (*She breaks down, sitting on the sofa and sobbing
  into her napkin*)
Vicar Most becoming, black, I think, to women. But alas so little oppor-
  tunity to wear it. Except for effect, of course. But that somewhat detracts
  from it. Oh well, we've done our best. We've done our best, dear lady,
  and we can't do more than that. She'll be in better hands than ours soon,
  infinitely better.

The bulldozers stop

Sally Hush, they've stopped. They must have got there, Simon.
Simon Well, time's getting on.
Maud (*looking out*) Shush.

They all listen, turned towards the window

*William comes in, in full uniform—Guards scarlet tunic, bearskin and
sword. He comes down the centre of the room*

William 'Morning, all.

*They all turn to look at William. Maud half rises, then sits again. Everyone
is nonplussed at the sight of William, and speechless*

I said good morning.
Maud 'Morning, William.
Vicar Good morning, Sir William.
Simon 'Morning, sir.
Sally Good morning, Grandpa.

William Touch of frost last night.

Vicar Seven degrees, Sir William.

William That much? Lucky the old girl had her grave dug on Saturday. Where's Robertson?

Sally He came in with the coffee, Grandpa.

William Should be on the lawn by now. Three minutes to. See if he's on the lawn, my boy.

Simon looks out of the window

Simon Yes, sir, he is.

William Good. Very glad you've turned out, Vicar. Hoped you would. The old girl's a churchwarden, after all. Well, getting on for zero hour.

The bulldozers start up

Sally They've started up their engines.

William Ninety seconds.

Hubert enters

Maud Hubert, did you talk to her?

Hubert I tried to. The door's locked. Have you talked to her this morning, Father?

The bulldozers start fading

William No—she wouldn't answer. Shouted through the dressing-room door, but she wasn't playing.

The bulldozers stop. The telephone rings. They all look at it. Hubert lifts the receiver

Hubert (*into the phone*) Hullo? . . . Oh, hullo, sir . . . Hold the line. (*To William*) It's for you, Father.

Vicar (*to William*) Telephone for you.

William What?

Vicar Telephone.

William Who for?

Vicar You, sir.

William Who from?

Hubert Sir Gerald, Father.

William Tell him I'll ring back later.

Hubert (*on the phone*) Hullo, sir. He'll ring you later . . . Hold on. I'll ask him. (*He puts his hand over the receiver*) He says, are you lunching with him or not, Father?

William (*breaking*) How should I know! How the hell should I know!

Hubert (*on the phone*) Hullo, sir. He'll call back later . . . Good-bye. (*He replaces the receiver*)

The bulldozers start up again, approaching

Simon They're moving again.

Simon and Sally look out of the window. Maud joins them, followed by Hubert and the Vicar

William Fifteen seconds.

The Vicar bows his head. The clock strikes in the hall. On the first stroke, the "Last Post" sounds. William draws his sword and stands at the salute, turned towards the window

> *After about half a minute, Sheila enters, wearing a housecoat. She pauses, watching the motionless tableau. No-one sees her as they stand with heads bowed, round the window*

Sheila sets two cups and pours coffee for herself and William, sitting down in her usual seat, which has not been used. She begins to help herself to toast and butter. The "Last Post" stops. The bulldozers continue. William cuts the salute, replaces his sword in its scabbard, takes off his bearskin and puts it on the piano

Oh well, that's that. We can all fall out now, thank God.

The bulldozers continue. The others turn away from the window. Hubert and the Vicar move to the desk. Maud sits and Sally comforts her. No-one yet looks at the breakfast table

William (*moving to sit in his usual place at the breakfast table*) Well, Robertson did the old girl proud, if you ask me . . . sugar please . . .

Sheila pushes the sugar basin across

. . . considering he hasn't sounded the damned thing for thirty years.
Sheila Yes, very nicely. Marmalade, please.

Maud screams and rises. Everybody swings round

Sally Grannie . . .
Vicar Lady Boothroyd!
Hubert Mother!
William Bless my soul, it's you. I thought I recognized your voice.
Sheila Good morning, everybody.

> *Robertson enters, wearing a khaki, balaclava-type woollen helmet and coney mittens, and carrying his bugle*

Robertson How was that, Sir William?
Sheila Good morning, Robertson.
Robertson (*automatically*) Good mor . . . (*Realizing*) Gawd! (*Recovering*) Good morning, my lady. So you thought you wouldn't, after all?
Sheila Well, who would, on a lovely morning like this? I do wish you'd all sit down. You make me nervous, standing staring at me. (*She rises and reassuringly pats William's hand*) 'Morning, everybody. (*She sits on the sofa*) Simon, be an angel and bring me my coffee.

Robertson hands Simon Sheila's coffee-cup. Sally sits by Sheila and puts her hands over hers emotionally

Sally Grannie . . .
Sheila Cheer up, dear. I won't take back the bracelet—or the necklace, Maud.
Hubert What happened, Mother?
Sheila Hubert, surely you're going to miss your train?
Hubert Yes, I suppose I ought to go.
Sheila Well, run along, dear. Don't let me detain you.
Robertson I'll get the car, sir.
Hubert Thank you, Robertson.

Robertson goes

Well, good-bye, Mother.
Sheila By the way, dear——

Hubert turns back

—about what you were shouting through the keyhole—I won't cut you off, if you don't cut off Sally.
Hubert Oh—well, thank you, Mother. Yes—well—so long, everybody. (*He shakes hands with Simon, then returns to kiss Sally*) Good-bye, Sally. (*He kisses Sheila*) Good-bye, Mother.
Sheila Good-bye, dear.
Hubert So long, Dad.
William (*thinking other thoughts*) 'Bye, Hubert.
Hubert (*patting his coat*) Well, I think that I've got everything.
Sheila What about Maud?
Maud Oh, yes! We've people lunching with us in the House of Commons.
Sheila Well, you're very suitably dressed.
Maud Good-bye, Sheila—thank you for the week-end.
Sheila Not at all, dear. It was very nice of you to come down. And I hope that you enjoyed it.
Maud Oh, yes.
Sally Good-bye, Mother.
Hubert Come along, Maud, or we'll miss the train.
Maud Yes, coming. (*Kissing Sally*) Good-bye, darling. (*To the Vicar*) Good-bye, Vicar. (*To Simon*) Good-bye. (*To William*) Good-bye, William.
Vicar Could I cadge a lift down to the vicarage? I'm late, too.
Hubert Of course.

Hubert and Maud exit

Vicar Thank you. Good-bye, Lady Boothroyd, and congratulations.
Sheila Good-bye, Vicar. It was kind of you to come.
Vicar No, not at all. The least that I could do. I'm so glad you decided to pay heed to my advice in the end, Lady Boothroyd.

Hubert returns

Hubert (*calling*) Vicar!

Hubert goes again

Vicar Yes. Good-bye, Sir William.
William Good-bye, Vicar.

The Vicar goes

Sally Grannie, did the Vicar really make you change your mind?
Sheila No.
Sally What did, then?
Sheila The thought of missing *Panorama*.
Sally Grannie!
Sheila It's true, dear.
Sally But you won't be on *Panorama* now you haven't done it.
Sheila Oh, dear, nor I will. I never thought of that. Perhaps I'd better reconsider.
Sally Don't be silly. Then you wouldn't see it, would you.
Sheila Nor I would. Well, let's forget it.
Sally Do you really mean that that was all that stopped you?
Sheila Not entirely, dear.

Robertson enters

Robertson There's seventeen reporters waiting in the drive, my lady, and they don't seem too pleased.
Sheila Poor things! They must be cold. Take them all into the billiard-room and give them whisky. Tell them I'll come along as soon as I'm dressed.
Robertson Very good, my lady.

Robertson exits

Simon gives Sheila her coffee

Simon (*feeling de trop*) I'll go and try to cheer them up while they're waiting.
Sheila Thank you, Simon.

Simon goes

Sally Sheila, I know why you didn't do it.
Sheila So do I, dear.
William Well, I'm damned if I do.
Sheila That's because you're not a woman, William.
Sally Women know when they're beaten, Grandpa—so they don't go on

and on being ridiculous through obstinacy, like men. That's right, Grannie, isn't it?

Sheila Perhaps, dear.

Sally (*also feeling de trop*) Well, I'll go and help with the drinks.

Sally goes

The sound of the bulldozers is heard again. William turns to look at Sheila, who averts her eyes and rises, moving towards the window with her cup in her hand. She looks out at the bulldozers, then puts the cup on the piano

William Sheila . . .

Sheila Yes?

William Was that the reason why you didn't do it—about women knowing when they're beaten?

Sheila No, dear.

William What the devil was it, then?

Sheila You, William.

William Me?

Sheila Yes, you. I couldn't bear to leave you.

William Don't be daft.

Sheila No, it's true, William. When I woke this morning and I heard you snoring in the dressing-room, I realized it for the first time. Oh, I loved you when I married you all right, until I met Tim Carson. But since then I've often thought how boring you were, with your deafness and your repetition, and your always saying "What?" It drove me to distraction, and the older that I got the more it drove me. (*She takes out a handkerchief*) Then this morning when I woke and heard you snoring, and I saw that photograph of you beside my bed—the one of you and Hubert when he was a baby—(*getting tearful*)—I just knew I couldn't leave you, at least not till God arranged things in his own good time. (*She turns up stage to blow her nose*) Stay with me, you darling old bore. Stay with me as long as possible.

There is no reaction from William

Have you been listening? Have you heard anything that I've been saying, William?

William Yes. What?

Sheila Never mind. I've got to talk to those poor, disappointed young men.

Sheila goes. William walks to the telephone and dials

William (*into the phone*) Hullo, Gerald? William here. The old girl's coming, after all.

William replaces the receiver, as—

the CURTAIN *falls*

FURNITURE AND PROPERTY LIST

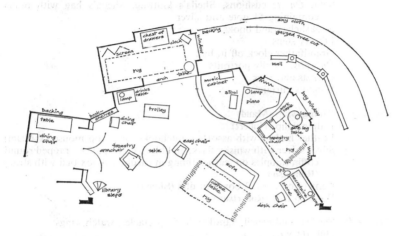

ACT I

SCENE 1

On stage: Baby grand piano. *On it:* book of Mozart sonatas, opened at K.331, "Funeral March" sheet, English hymnal. *On lid:* lamp, dressing, photograph groups, ashtrays, etc.

Piano stool.

Desk. *On it:* wicker cage with budgerigar, glass jug of water, birdseed, lamp. *In pigeon-holes:* cheque-book, envelopes, dressing. *On writing flap:* telephone, assorted bills, writing materials, notebook, blotter, small wooden tray with salmon-fly vice, mounted on a teabox, set on it. Partly made "Hairy Mary" fly set in vice, with reels of silks, assorted feathers, a squirrel tail and pair of small scissors on tray. *On floor:* waste-paper basket

Desk chair

Circular table with cloth. *On it:* 2 places set with 2 side-plates, knives, egg-spoons, napkins in silver rings, marmalade, butter, sugar basin, salt, pepper, extra napkin for Hubert

Breakfast trolley. *On it:* cloths, the *Advertiser* newspaper, coffee-pot and coffee, milk jug and milk, letter from Gerald, knives, 6 cups, 6 saucers, 6 spoons, pile of small plates with knife and egg-spoon on top, pile of napkins, 2 boiled eggs in cosies, silver eggstand with boiled eggs

Coffee-table
2 occasional tables with photographs, lamps
Music cabinet with sheet music on shelves
Work table
2 tapestry armchairs
Easy chair
Dining chair
Sofa. *On it:* cushions, Sheila's knitting, Sheila's bag with purse
    containing £1 note and silver
Bookshelves and books
Library steps
Grandfather clock off in hall
On walls: family portraits
Carpets and rugs
Window curtains

Off stage: Riding whip (**Maud**)
    Riding whip (**Hubert**)
    Leather hatbox with assorted notebooks and prop mouse (**William**)
    Silver salver with whisky flask, and black crêpe paper wrapped round
        coffin samples on leather thong in cardboard box tied with string
        (**Robertson**)
    Camera on cord, 3 boxes of film (**Simon**)
    Wooden tray (**Robertson**)

Personal: **Sheila:** gold pencil, handkerchief, spectacles, watch, rings
    Hubert: wristwatch
    William: pocket watch

Scene 2

Strike: Notebooks from hatbox
    Cups and saucers
    Empty sample box
    Newspaper
    Trolley
    Breakfast table

Set: Hatbox (open) and knitting to hide Sheila's bag on sofa
    Large brown envelope, cardboard tombstone cut-out with inscrip-
        tions and scissors on sofa table
    Bowl of primroses on piano
    Bowl of primroses and trug basket with daffodils, fork and trowel,
        on occasional table
    Trick crocus bowl on sofa table
    Cushions tidy
    Grandfather clock to 10.20

Off stage: Sunday newspapers in a pile arranged as follows:
        Top: *Sunday Express* with special heading
        2nd: *Sunday Times* without supplement

3rd: *Observer* without supplement
4th: *News of the World*
Supplements and *Times* magazine
Sunday Mirror and *People* (all for **Robertson**)
Handbag with handkerchief, Prayer Book **(Maud)**
Sunday Telegraph **(Simon)**

ACT II

SCENE 1

Strike: Dining chair
All newspapers
Hatbox
Trug basket
Scissors
Large brown envelope
Broken piece of china from crocus bowl

Set: Curtains closed
Grandfather clock to 9.10
Knitting, Sheila's bag, and Maud's handbag with handkerchief on
sofa
Silver coffee tray with 5 coffee-cups, 5 saucers, 5 spoons, silver cream
jug with cream, silver sugar basin with sugar, silver coffee-pot with
coffee, on sofa table
Desk and cushions tidy

Off stage: *News of the World* refolded to outer pages **(Robertson)**
Large pile of William's notebooks **(Simon)**
Silver tray with decanter of whisky, 5 glasses, soda syphon in silver
stand **(Robertson)**

Personal: **Sheila:** pearl necklace, ear-rings, emerald bracelet, spectacles on
cord
Hubert: filled pipe

SCENE 2

Strike: Maud's handbag and *News of the World*
Coffee tray
Dirty glasses

Set: Window curtains open
Breakfast table as in Act I
Easy chair and tapestry chair on either side of it
Dining chair above it
Trolley as in Act I. *On it:* butter dish and knife, marmalade and spoon,

sugar basin and tongs, silver cruets, empty egg cosy, empty napkin ring, side-plate with egg in silver egg-cup and egg-spoon, pile
of small plates, 6 cups, 6 saucers, 6 spoons, side-plate with knife
on it, milk in jug, fresh coffee in pot
Knitting on sofa
Grandfather clock to 7.40
Cushions tidy

Off stage: Bugle, khaki scarf, mittens (**Robertson**)
Toast-rack with fresh toast (**Robertson**)

Personal: **Sheila:** handkerchief in dressing-gown pocket
Hubert: watch
Robertson: watch
Simon: watch

LIGHTING PLOT

Property fittings required: table lamps, chandelier
Interior. A living-room. The same scene throughout

ACT I, SCENE 1. Morning
To open: Effect of morning light
Cue 1   **Hubert** enters   (Page 4)
             Slow increase of general lighting

ACT I, SCENE 2. Morning
To open: As end of Cue 1
No cues

ACT II, SCENE 1. Evening
To open: All lamps and chandelier on
No cues

ACT II, SCENE 2. Morning
To open: Effect of dull, early morning light
Cue 2   **Vicar:** ". . . infinitely better."   (Page 45)
             Slow increase of general lighting

EFFECTS PLOT

ACT I

SCENE 1

Cue 1   **Sheila** finishes playing scales   (Page   1)
              Grandfather clock strikes eight

SCENE 2

Cue 2   **Sheila:** ". . . to Transport House, then."   (Page 27)
              Church bell tolls for matins

Cue 3   Robertson enters with the *Sunday Mirror*   (Page 28)
              Bells stop

Cue 4   **Sally:** "Oh, that's marvellous."   (Page 29)
              Telephone rings

Cue 5   **Hubert:** ". . . up the Solent with a friend."   (Page 29)
              Single bell tolls

Cue 6   **Sheila:** "Quite right."   (Page 30)
              Telephone rings. Single bell stops

ACT II

SCENE 1

Cue 7   **William:** ". . . Three-no-trumps."   (Page 37)
              Telephone rings

Cue 8   **William:** ". . . just as they were going to plant it."   (Page 39)
              Telephone rings

SCENE 2

Cue 9   **Robertson:** ". . . thirty years."   (Page 42)
              Bulldozers start in distance and continue

Cue 10   **Simon:** ". . . read his diaries."   (Page 43)
              Bulldozers swell, then fade, and continue

Cue 11   **Maud:** "No, not . . ."   (Page 45)
            Bulldozers swell, then fade, and continue

Cue 12   **Simon:** ". . . in his bath just now."   (Page 45)
            Bulldozers swell, then fade, and continue

Cue 13   **Vicar:** ". . . somewhat detracts from it."   (Page 45)
            Bulldozers swell, then continue

Cue 14   **Vicar:** ". . . soon, infinitely better."   (Page 45)
            Bulldozers stop

Cue 15   **William:** ". . . getting on for zero hour."   (Page 46)
            Bulldozers start up

Cue 16   **William:** ". . . she wasn't playing."   (Page 46)
            Telephone rings. Bulldozers stop

Cue 17   **Hubert:** "He'll call back later . . . Good-bye."   (Page 46)
            Bulldozers start up again, approaching

Cue 18   **William:** "Fifteen seconds."   (Page 47)
            After count of 3, grandfather clock strikes 8

Cue 19   As clock starts to strike   (Page 47)
            "Last Post" sounds, then bulldozers continue

Cue 20   **Sally** exits   (Page 50)
            Bulldozers swell up, fade as **Sheila** *puts cup on piano, then*
                continue till end of play

DATE DUE